A History of Women's Lives in Coventry

A History of Women's Lives in Coventry

Cathy Hunt

First published in Great Britain in 2018
by Pen & Sword HISTORY
An imprint of Pen & Sword Books Limited
47 Church Street, Barnsley, South Yorkshire, S70 2AS

ISBN 9781526708502

A CIP catalogue record for this book is available from the British Library.

Typeset in 11.5/13.5 point Times NR MT by SRJ Info Jnana System Pvt Ltd.

Printed and bound in England by TJ International Ltd.

Pen & Sword Books Limited incorporates the imprints of Atlas,
Archaeology, Aviation, Discovery, Family History, Fiction, History, Maritime,
Military, Military Classics, Politics, Select, Transport, True Crime, Air World,
Frontline Publishing, Leo Cooper, Remember When, Seaforth Publishing,
The Praetorian Press, Wharncliffe Local History, Wharncliffe Transport,
Wharncliffe True Crime and White Owl.

For a complete list of Pen & Sword titles please contact
PEN & SWORD BOOKS LIMITED
47 Church Street, Barnsley, South Yorkshire S70 2AS, United Kingdom
email enquiries@pen-and-sword.co.uk
www.pen-and-sword.co.uk

Contents

Acknowledgements

Special thanks to all at Coventry History Centre for their expert help and for granting permission to use photographs. Thanks also to the Herbert Art Gallery and Museum for allowing me access to photographs from the museum's collections and special thanks to Ali Wells for her help with this. David Fry has shared his knowledge of Coventry's history with me and I would like to record my thanks to him for his generosity in letting me use so many images from his collection. Thanks also to John Biddle, Ann Callow, Albert Smith, Megan Saxelby and Enid Trent and her family for use of their photographs.

Thank you to Lynn Hockton for advice, suggestions and excellent proof reading and to Mary and Len Hunt for readings. To Rachel Field, with whom I have had so many wonderful conversations about women's lives and who gave much indexing help. Lastly, thank you to Bill for his continued love and support.

I have made every effort to ensure that there are no breaches of copyright within the book. If any errors in this respect are found, please contact me via Pen and Sword Books Ltd.

This book is for the women of Coventry but it is dedicated to my mother, Sheila Gibbons, who has this year made Coventry her home.

Introduction

There are plenty of histories of Coventry, but this one focuses entirely on the lives of the women who lived here. In the hundred years covered, from 1850 to 1950, many women from the city achieved fame in their chosen fields and others were pioneers, breaking through barriers and paving the way for future generations of Coventry women to experience greater political, economic and social freedoms than had been possible for their mothers. While the importance and significance of the work of these women is undisputed, the main focus of this book is on the daily lives of women, on what it was like to grow up in Coventry, to go to its schools, to work in its offices, shops and factories, to set up home, to get married and have a family, to rest when time allowed or to offer time and talent for the good of the community.

In 1851 Coventry's population was 36,812. The city centre, hemmed in by lands where development was at that time prohibited, was overcrowded and too many people lived in inadequate housing and contracted diseases born of poor public health which led to premature deaths. The development of suburbs outside the centre was slow and slum clearance even slower. In 1889 Coventry's overall death rate was 17.5 per 1,000 of the population, with the Medical Officer of Health noting that 'the number of old-fashioned, unwholesome dwellings, crowded into courts and yards off the older streets, is too large to allow of a model death rate'. The infant mortality rate, at 150 per 1,000 births was over eight times higher than this, with many deaths from, for example, bronchitis, inflammation of the lungs, diarrhoea and prematurity, regarded by the Medical Officer as largely preventable.

Coventry in 1910, just over half way through our period. The view shows Priory Row in the foreground, with the ground sloping away to Pool Meadow, with Hillfields and Foleshill to the north. *Courtesy of Coventry History Centre.*

By 1951 Coventry's population was 258,245 and infant mortality had significantly decreased. Every citizen had the right to free medical care and there was a social security safety net to eliminate the worst of poverty. Instead of the large families common in the nineteenth century, the typical family unit was made up of just two children. Wages were higher and employment plentiful but we must be careful not to assume that this meant progress for all. Homelessness was a serious problem for many in Coventry after the Second World War, with families camped out in former hostels, parks and on bomb sites.

The industrial base of the city had been transformed from a nineteenth-century one dependent on the craft industries of silk ribbon weaving and the manufacture of clocks and watches, to one centred on the motor industry, machine tools and engineering. Four boundary extensions between 1890 and 1932 accounted for some of the population growth but there were also surges due to migration to take advantage of the availability of jobs and relatively good wages and the city's population was growing at a rate seven times higher than the country as a whole. From 1931 to 1940, when the city's population was 229,500, the growth rate was thirty six per cent. In order to accommodate such a phenomenal rise, a vast amount of houses were built for Coventry kids and newcomers alike.

The hundred years saw economic boom times and devastating crashes, unemployment and poverty, years of prosperity and years of war. All of these contributed to the unique character and spirit of Coventry, which attracted so much attention in the days after its devastating pounding by enemy aircraft in November 1940 and again in April 1941. Through all of these changes, women were depended upon by fathers, husbands and children to provide stability and support. Despite legal changes and greater opportunities in education and professional work, there was a continued expectation that married women would stay at home, raise the children and be the moral and domestic lynchpin of the family. Men, it was assumed, would provide for them financially and protect them from the need to do anything other than care for the family.

The reality was, of course, very different and this is one of the reasons why it is so important to have a women's history of Coventry, to remind us never to generalise about women's lives. Coventry was a predominately working-class city and its largest industries were male dominated, with women workers paid less and, in some factories, expected – or forced – to leave when they got married. But some women remained single, others were widowed or divorced; they had different hopes, needs, ambitions and incomes. Women were also depended upon by employers and by the state; this was particularly evident in the First and Second World Wars when their labour was needed in the country's factories, on the land, in the hospitals and in the Services. When war was over, women were expected to return to their traditional domestic roles and concentrate all their efforts on motherhood. Yet for many, the tragedies of war made this impossible, while others had no intention of taking up such work, instead seeking independence and fulfilment outside the home.

It can be difficult to find out about the lives of ordinary women who, by and large, were too busy to keep diaries and even those who did, did not always consider them important enough to preserve. Material may be unevenly spread out but it is there, in the form of minutes, log-books, newspapers and censuses and in the meticulous and detailed research of others. Special mentions here must go to the Coventry History Centre's oral history collection. This provided me with access to the voices and recollections of Coventry women who lived through the early twentieth century, the inter-war and war years. Some of the accounts are anonymous, accounting for my frequent use of the phrase, 'one Coventry woman recalled…', but where possible, I have referred to women by name.

A young Coventry woman, photographed in the 1890s. *Courtesy of the Herbert Art Gallery & Museum, Coventry*

Since 1998, the Coventry Women's Research Group has researched and written about many aspects of women's lives

New horizons: Coventry women on holiday between the wars. *Courtesy of Albert Smith*

in the city and their numerous publications provide accessible detail and form an invaluable resource for historians. I have drawn on some of the stories that they have collected and here record my gratitude to those who researched and collected these wonderful accounts of lives which were never ordinary.

I am one of the many incomers whom Coventry has welcomed. Thirty-seven years ago I came to the city from another part of the country, joining many others from all over the world who are proud to have made Coventry their home. I have raised my children here, worked here and have come to realise how much I have in common with those women who have gone before me. As I write this, I have dashed out into the garden several times to rescue the washing from the spring showers. For years, my working day was punctuated by planning family meals, shopping, cooking, washing and cleaning. Sure, I have devices to help me do the latter that my great-grandmothers could not have dreamed of, but the thinking and the organising are, I suspect, largely unaltered. I have had greater opportunities than my grandmothers in education, work and travel. I have experienced better housing, more comforts and – so far – better health than they did. My children were delivered safely in hospital and I received maternity pay giving me the option of time at home to recover and spend time with my babies, whose chances of surviving childhood were enormously higher than they were throughout the whole period covered in this book. Life for women in 2018, the year that we celebrate one hundred years of (limited) women's suffrage, has, in many ways, become easier, yet there is a long way to go. On the whole, women are still paid less than men and they are over represented in the country's lowest paid jobs. It is still assumed that child care is a woman's responsibility, yet full-time mothers are as likely to be criticised by the press as those who return to work after maternity leave.

This, then, is a book about change but also one about continuity. I am conscious that in a work of this length, I have not been able to cover every aspect of being a woman in Coventry over the hundred year period, but I hope that I am able to give some indication of life in this city from women's perspective. For those who are disappointed that I have referred too briefly to Coventry in the Second World War and the post-war years, I invite you to read some of the wonderful accounts that already exist about this period, many of which can be found in the bibliography to this book. To those of you who lived through these years, I urge you to talk and write about them so that others can learn your stories too.

I offer this, my contribution to the city's history, to all the women who have made a difference, those who have led, cared and inspired – the politicians, professionals, volunteers and mothers and daughters everywhere.

CHAPTER ONE

Learning for Life

From 1911 Angela Brazil lived at number One, The Quadrant, in the centre of Coventry and enjoyed enormous success as a writer of schoolgirl fiction. In her books, with titles such as *For the Sake of the School* and *A Patriotic Schoolgirl,* girls formed lasting friendships and had spirited adventures in the best days of their lives at small, intimate boarding schools where the best teachers could be stern but were ultimately just, kind and motherly. The appeal of these books was, for most girls, surely in their depiction of a safe world, in which girls were involved in no end of scrapes but ultimately protected from life's harshest realities.

Our hundred-year period highlights great differences in women's experiences of education. In 1950 the main problems facing Coventry's Education Department were how to accommodate rising numbers of pupils in a city where school buildings had been badly damaged during the Second World War and how to restore order and continuity for children whose schooling had been disrupted by the strains of war. In 1850 there was no local authority provision but a muddle of schools offering education of varying quality, making it almost impossible to monitor how many children attended regularly, if at all. Parents, then as now, wanted to do what was best for their children but for so many families in Coventry, formal education was often interrupted or cut short by the need to make ends meet.

For the greater part of the nineteenth century, there was no unified system of education in Britain. The schooling that you received depended very much on where you lived and what class and circumstances you were born into. It was not until the Education Act of 1870 that an attempt was made to ensure the widespread and consistent provision of elementary education. Because school attendance was not compulsory until 1880 and not free until 1891, many children were still unable to take full advantage of the learning opportunities available. Crucially, depending on personal circumstances, learning was also heavily influenced by whether you were a boy or a girl. One of the prevailing ideas in Victorian society was that of separate spheres for the sexes, placing men in the roles of breadwinner, provider and protector, and women in those of nurturer and home maker – the famous angel of hearth and home. Despite the fact that the realities of life made a nonsense of this ideology for those women who had no choice but to seek paid work, its influences were apparent in virtually all types of educational provision, no matter what class you were born into.

Nineteenth-century education in Coventry

In the early 1850s a series of articles in the Coventry *Herald* declared that more than two thirds of the children in the city, 'in the centre of civilized England,' did not attend school and as a result, were growing up in 'heathen ignorance of the commonest elements of knowledge', condemned 'to more or less of mental darkness, premature labour, street idling, early depravity or worldly hardiness'. These reports condemned much of the teaching in the city as inadequate and concluded that Coventry needed to double the number of schools and treble the number of efficient teachers. The newspaper, owned and edited by local ribbon manufacturer, philanthropist and self-styled philosopher, Charles Bray, reflected middle-class concerns that even in what were considered to be the best of the schools on offer, classes were too big and pupils attended for too short a time before they had to leave to enter the world of employment.

Among the schools reckoned to be the worst in the city were the 'dame schools', so-called because they were often run by women, set up in poor parts of towns and villages, with low fees. Many with an interest in children's education, such as Bray, were quick to dismiss these as inferior institutions run by incompetent women, caring only about making a living. His newspaper said that the schools were 'kept by persons of inferior education' and standards of teaching were presumed to be low, with emphasis on little more than spelling and basic arithmetic, particularly as some working parents regarded teachers as little more than child minders for the very youngest pupils. But it would be a mistake to regard all dame schools in this light; many children did learn and were cared for with kindness and gentleness by intelligent, thoughtful women who would have undertaken training if they had access to it.

Charity and Industrial Schools

Among the 'best' schools referred to by the *Herald* were those known as gift or charity schools, where poor boys were 'gifted' an apprenticeship into a trade after a few years of schooling and where the emphasis on girls' education was on what was deemed to be most necessary for them to know – their place in life, as servants, and ultimately as wives and mothers. Circumstances had to be pretty dire for this type of 'rescue' to be available to children and in Coventry there were more places for boys than for girls at such schools. Blue Coat, adjacent to Holy Trinity Church in the centre of Coventry was one such charity school, founded in 1714 and maintained by regular public subscription. In the nineteenth century, regular 'Blue Coat Sundays' at Holy Trinity urged congregations to support the school's aims – to educate fifty poor girls of the city in the principles of the church, to clothe them, supply books and instruct them in the various branches of domestic industry, including sewing, washing and cooking. One of the traditions of the school was that the six eldest girls would live and work there, under the instruction of the Matron who would train and prepare them for domestic service.

Bluecoat School girls, in their distinctive uniform, walking from the school in Priory Row to Holy Trinity Church. *Courtesy of Coventry History Centre*

The preserved exercise books of Blue Coat girl Rosa Atkins show that in 1871, she was learning how to sort a household's linen ready for washing:

> I must first collect both the sheets, towels, pillowcases and soiled clothes from the bags in the bedrooms; all the gowns, petticoats, chemises, handkerchiefs, caps, shirts, collars, cravats, waistcoats, light trousers and stockings, all the table cloths, dinner napkins, coarse cloths and towels from the kitchen and throw them on the floor of the room used for that purpose.

She demonstrated her knowledge of daily duties from early morning – 'unfasten the doors and open the window shutters … light the parlour fires … prepare the breakfast for the family' through the day until evening – 'I go upstairs, turn down the beds, draw the curtains, close the windows and put everything in order in the bedrooms'. When she had eaten her own tea, '… if I have any time to spare, I employ it in repairing any clothes and keeping them in a proper state'. Asked if that was all for the day, she wrote that all that now remained was 'to prepare and take up the supper tray and remove it when done with and before I go to bed, to see that all the lights and fires are extinguished'.

While an education at Blue Coat may have been a lifeline to orphaned girls or those whose families were in dire straits, not all parents accepted that it served their daughters' best interests. In the early twentieth century, May Purnell was taken away from the school by her mother at the point when her domestic training was due to begin and sent to an elementary Council school. As a domestic at Coventry and Warwickshire Hospital, her mother had already seen 'that side of life' herself and was adamant that it was not what she wanted for her daughters. At her new school (Cheylesmore), May felt more relaxed about learning in a freer environment, where she likened the wonders of learning history to listening to fairy stories. While she recognised that the Blue Coat girls made a pretty sight in their distinctive, old-fashioned uniforms, walking between the school and Holy Trinity next door, she didn't like wearing it because it marked her out as a charity pupil. Mrs Masterman, a Blue Coat pupil between 1928 and 1934, recalled the serge dress, which, covered with a pinafore, had to last all through the winter without being washed. The summer dresses were made of cotton and the girls had a clean one each week. The black stockings and lace up boots, worn all year, were hard to bear, while she shuddered when thinking back on the underclothes.

Blue Coat also came under the category of 'industrial' school, because it prepared girls 'in the department of female industry' and it was joined in 1865 by Sir Thomas White's School on Stoney Stanton Road, offering places to boarders and day girls. In addition to these schools was Coventry's Certified Industrial School and Home in Leicester Street, where some girls were sent by magistrates, simply because there was nowhere else for them to go. Some of these came to Coventry from other areas; in 1896 8-year-old Maud was sent to the Home from Hereford to remain until she was 16. According to the admission notes, her mother, a charwoman and reputed prostitute, had been sent to prison for neglect of her children while her father, a joiner, had sailed for America some years earlier and was thought to be dead. While Maud's character was judged to be 'good', 13-year-old Elizabeth from London was considered 'uncontrollable' and

Pupils at Sir Thomas White's School, 1918. The girls educated here between 1865 and 1919 were the orphaned daughters of Coventry Freeman (those who had completed apprenticeships within the city). Preparation in domestic work was a central part of the curriculum. *Courtesy of David Fry*

with 'a tendency for immorality'. Her mother was a workhouse inmate and her father in prison for deserting his family. In 1908 7-year-old Ellen had been found 'wandering'. Her father was described as a drunken loafer, her mother as a prostitute, in prison for drunkenness. Character judgements of other girls included 'wild' or just plain 'bad'. Life at the Home was never easy for the girls; in 1893 the Home Office was called to investigate an allegation of excessive and degrading physical punishment given to a girl in full view of the other children by the superintendent. The girl had been accused of taking some of the bread and treacle she was preparing, giving some to another girl and eating some herself. The superintendent resigned, claiming that she was not aware of the Home's rules that forbade corporal punishment in public. It seems that had she used a birch instead of a cane and had she done so in private, the matter would have been of no concern to anyone (other than the

Girls' Industrial Home, Leicester Street. This building, on the site of the previous home, opened in 1889. *Courtesy of David Fry*

girl who endured the pain and humiliation of the caning). There seems, however, to have been public support for the superintendent; a July letter to the *Coventry Herald* written by a gentleman in London declared his incomprehension that 'punishment to a boy by a master in the presence of boys should constantly take place without notice and the same punishment to a girl by a matron in the presence of girls should be complained of'. As a result he resolved never to subscribe a penny to any girls' industrial school where the matron's hands were so tied 'from giving corporal punishment to girls who are utterly uncontrollable except by this means as a reserve and last resort'.

Attendance and Hard Times

For those muddling through, keeping their heads above water in a city used to peaks and troughs in its dominant industry of ribbon weaving, children might attend a school provided by one of two societies – the National, run by the Church of England and the British and Foreign, organised by the non-denominational churches. By the middle of the nineteenth century Coventry had seventeen such schools and its teachers received their training through the Home and Colonial Scheme, and were among those the *Herald* believed were the 'pioneers of a new race of educators'. Such schools aimed at providing a good grounding in the 'Three Rs' (reading, writing and arithmetic); at the National Society's St Michael's Infant School in Much Park Street, the teacher, Miss Cox, was regarded as an excellent teacher, well qualified for her work. Classes were large, with little or no time to offer individual attention. Teachers relied on monitors, usually the most senior and ablest pupils, to teach by rote.

A major problem was that attendance was not free; the National and British schools charged between 2*d* and 4*d* a week. In 1862 a factory inspector in the Midlands complained of the negligence and improvidence of parents who did not send their children to school, when a working man could educate his family of six for 18*d* a week. But there lay the problem for many Coventry families. In 1857 Charles Bray noted that watchmakers aimed to keep their children at school until they were 14, but things were less stable in the ribbon trade. When trade was good, a weaver might be able to afford to send his children to school, but if he rented or owned his own loom, the entire family was needed to assist with the weaving processes and to run errands. From the age of 8, children were regarded as ready to assist their parents. During regular slumps and periods of unemployment in the trade, the sparing of cash to send children to school became impossible. In 1873, the Spon Street School log-book recorded that 'none of the children previously admitted made their appearance, probably on account of the parents' inability to pay the fees'. When, from 1891, fees were no longer payable, Miss Selina Dix, at that time headmistress of South Street Girls' School gathered her pupils together and told them that they would no longer have to bring in money each week to attend school, urging them instead to pay the money into a savings bank or a clothing club.

It was far more common for girls to be kept from school than boys, to help with all the chores of the household, in times of sickness, childbirth or parental absence. This was not peculiar to the ribbon industry but simply what was expected of girls. In the 1890s, the South Street School log-book, noted that a list of the 'most hardened absentees' had been drawn up so that parents could receive warnings. It was alleged that mothers who were constantly 'sending for' their daughters were blaming their absences on the need to go out to work in hard times, relying on the older daughters to care for the younger children. In 1897 'an unpleasant interview' with 'an insolent woman' who kept her child at home about twice every week ended when the woman announced that she should 'keep her when she liked' and left the room.

In September 1896 the log-book recorded that cheap train excursions from Coventry were encouraging some mothers to take day trips to London or Birmingham and taking their daughters out of school to hold the fort until they got back. Girls learned early that they, more than their brothers, were expected to help with the family. One Coventry woman recalled that during the inter-war years, she was always late for school because she had to take her father's breakfast – a bacon sandwich and a can of tea – to the works at nine o'clock in the morning. On washing day (Monday), when she came home from school for lunch, she was required to lend a hand, scrubbing her father's collars and cuffs, always filthy from his work in the foundry.

As more ribbon factories were established in Coventry, competing with the artisans working from home, employers were swift to employ children because they could pay them less than adult workers and struggling families were grateful for the chance given to their offspring to contribute to the family income. Factory Acts forbade the employment of children under 9 and insisted that factory owners allowed children aged between 9 and 13 access to part time schooling. The regime of learning the ropes at work and also sitting through lessons at school (not to mention helping in the home) must have been exhausting, and it was noted by the head teacher at Spon Street School in 1873 that the half timers put in irregular appearances and were often late. Among the full time scholars, a factory inspector commented in 1862 that there were still too many parents who thought that they were 'conferring a favour on those who take an interest in their children in permitting them to attend school at all'!

Those children who could not be spared from contributing to the family income might be able to go to Sunday school, of which there were several attached to the city's churches. In 1851, the *Herald*, although of the firm opinion that Sunday attendance was meant to supplement and not replace going to a day school, cautioned that it was 'better that the child should receive some knowledge of reading and writing in one day of the week, but still we must not call this education'. Such concerns were shared by the founders of the Ragged Schools, offering day, evening and Saturday classes for children (and sometimes adults) who had no chance even to go to Sunday School and were perhaps beneath the attention of those regarded as being worthy of rescue and placed in the charity schools. From 1847, Coventry's Ragged School ran classes in various locations and by 1872 there was a separate girls' school in St Nicholas Street, where learning focused on the Three Rs, sewing and, of course, domestic or 'industrial' training. There is no mistaking the moral and religious objectives of the School – and its opinion of those who came to it – when in 1897, its organisers recalled that,

> Nothing was made so clear in the early days of [the school's] work as the evils wrought by the power of Satan over those whose intellect was dormant and their hearts resting in a false peace and security, and where temporal matters of time, in a depraved form, overshadowed and clouded any gleam of brightness for eternity.

For families facing the worst of times, the workhouse was often their only refuge. From 1844 Coventry Workhouse, at the city

STONELEIGH HOUSE,

GREY FRIARS' GREEN,

COVENTRY.

THE MISSES ABRAHAMS

AND

MISS ARCULUS

Undertake the Care and Tuition of Young Ladies, and instruct them in every branch of a sound ENGLISH EDUCATION, assisted by resident English and Foreign Governesses.

TERMS & REFERENCES ON APPLICATION TO THE PRINCIPAL.

Advertisement for a school for middle class girls, *Coventry Directory 1879. Courtesy of Coventry History Centre* end of London Road, appointed a schoolmaster and mistress to teach its young inmates. These children did at least receive a free education, and arguably one of better academic quality than many outside the workhouse were given, but it came at a heavy price to youngsters who were also expected to perform a wealth of domestic chores within the workhouse and who were largely separated from their families. From the late nineteenth century, there was a move to send the children to the local school instead, amid a growing belief that the atmosphere in the workhouse was damaging to impressionable young people. In 'Hurdy Gurdy Days', a wonderfully honest and vivid account of poverty in early twentieth century Coventry, published by the Coventry Women's Research Group, the narrator describes the workhouse children who attended her school, St Michael's in central Coventry. These 'half-starved, ill-mannered children who nobody wanted' were seated together, away from the other pupils, arriving at school with shaved heads to keep them clear of lice. They were dressed in rough, poor clothing, nervous and then yelled at by the teacher when they faced the consequences of lacking the courage to ask to go to the toilet. I wonder which was harder to bear – the discipline of the workhouse regime or the humiliation of being known as a workhouse kid at the local school?

Middle-class Girls

While a national system of elementary and then secondary education was taking shape in Britain, many middle-class parents continued to place their faith in forms of education that they believed were most suitable to their daughters' station in life. After being in the care of a governess for a few years, boys were soon packed off to boarding schools, where discipline was often extreme but educational standards more or less sufficient to prepare them to take their place in the public world of commerce, industry or the professions. The emphasis in middle-class girls' schooling was on turning out young ladies who knew just enough to make them intelligent companions to their husbands (while deferring to his superior knowledge) and – before that and most important of all – charming enough to ensure that they would marry – and marry well. While working-class girls were learning how to become servants, middle-class girls were learning how to behave in the manner expected of them by society. Parents wanted their daughters to become 'accomplished' – to be able to entertain evening guests with a little singing and piano playing, to show off their education by dropping a few pretty French phrases into polite conversation now and again, to sketch and to embroider.

There were no guarantees of a sound academic education for those girls who were sent to day or boarding schools. The novelist George Eliot (born Mary Ann Evans in 1819, near Nuneaton) attended the Misses Franklin's School in Coventry's Warwick Row from the age of 12. She was lucky; this was reckoned to be one of the best schools in Warwickshire and here, under the tutelage of the daughters of the local Baptist minister (regarded by Eliot's biographer as being 'the last word in female charm and culture'), she thrived. At thirty guineas a year for boarders, it was out of the price range of working-class parents but it was cheap compared to some establishments; as a child, social reformer Frances Power Cobbe was sent to a finishing school in Brighton in the 1830s costing £1,000 a year and which was, she later declared, completely lacking in intellectual stimulation. In 1844, the Misses Franklin, whose school was by now housed in Little Park Street, were careful to advertise that while their course of instruction offered some attention to the Sciences and Modern Languages, there was 'a primary regard to the formation of the character' and attention paid to 'the ornamental departments of a young Lady's Education'.

While she gained knowledge and experience at her Coventry school, there was to be no typical provincial ladyhood for George Eliot, whose unorthodox life as a writer set her apart from most of the pupils who attended schools for young ladies. The description of Rosamond Vincy's schooling in Eliot's 1871 novel *Middlemarch* (based on 1820s Coventry) appears to parody the Franklin sisters' advertisement. Rosamond, daughter of

Number 29, Warwick Row, where George Eliot attended the Misses Franklin's School from the age of twelve to sixteen. *Courtesy of Coventry History Centre*

a ribbon manufacturer, had been 'the flower of Mrs Lemon's school, the chief school in the county, where the teaching included all that was demanded in the accomplished female – even to extras, such as the getting in and out of a carriage'.

With her 'excellent taste in costume, with that nymph-like figure and pure blondness which gave her the largest range to choice in the flow and colour of drapery', Rosamond could not be exceeded 'for mental acquisition and propriety of speech, while her musical execution was quite exceptional'. She was, in other words, an asset to her family to be shown off at every possible opportunity and then to attract a suitable husband.

In 1868 the national Taunton Commission into education found fault with boys' and girls' schools but was particularly damning of those provided for girls, concluding that here there was a 'want of thoroughness and foundation, want of system; slovenliness and showy superficiality; inattention to rudiments; undue time to accomplishments, and those not taught intelligently or in any scientific manner'. Coventry newspapers ran advertisements for several private girls' schools, including the Misses Caporn of Greyfriars Green, Mrs Walters in Union Street, Miss Hives of Stoke Green and the Misses Kennedy and Hutchinson in College House, King Street, who, in 1871, offered French, German and Latin to their day and boarding pupils. Many such schools responded to campaigns to improve the quality of girls' education and by the early twentieth century, the (private) High School for Girls, run by Miss Hales in The Quadrant, was preparing pupils for public examinations and was inspected annually by University Inspectors. There were schoolmistresses for drawing, classics and history, modern languages, science, English and mathematics. Of those boarding in 1911, between the ages of 12 and 17, only one was from Warwickshire while others came from as far away as Jersey and York.

School Boards and Council Schools

The 1870 Education Elementary Act created School Boards across the country. Under these, existing schools were supervised and inspected and new ones established where there was need. In Coventry the first two Board Schools to open were Spon Street and South Street in the 1870s, followed by three more in

South Street Board School for Girls, 1886. The girls are with their head teacher, Miss Selina Dix (centre) and assistant teacher, Miss Webb. *Courtesy of Coventry History Centre*

the 1890s – Wheatley Street, Paradise and Red Lane. When the School Boards were abolished in 1902, the schools – and those established afterwards – became known as Council schools and were run by the local authority education department for pupils up to the age of 14. The main focus in the schools was on the Three Rs, plus needlework for girls.

The head teachers of the Board Schools battled with erratic attendance but also, when schools were full, with all the attendant disciplinary and health problems of overcrowding and inadequate classrooms. Frustration is apparent in the May 1879 entry in the Spon Street Girls' School log book when one class was taught in the playground and another in the passage way as, 'the schoolroom is really much too full now that the weather is getting warm. Have refused admittance to several children this week'. In June a mother came into school to ask if she could keep her daughter at home as she was unfit for school work; a

Wheatley Street Board (and then Council) School, which opened in 1893.
Courtesy of David Fry

doctor had attributed her illness to the overcrowded classroom. The young apprentice teachers were struggling to maintain order in crowded rooms and 'were making efforts to improve it' but it was an uphill task. Despite the difficulties, standards at the school were rising; in 1878 the government report was critical:

> The Singing is hardly up to the mark and will I hope improve. The Discipline and Needlework are very fair. The weak place in the elementary subjects is the Writing of the Third Standard and the Arithmetic of the Fourth. The children in the Third Standard showed want of intelligence throughout, their Geography being very indifferent. The extra subjects with this exception were fairly done.

By the next year, the girls did not disappoint; their 'singing has improved greatly, it is now tuneful and lively' and the elementary subjects as a whole were very fairly done, with grammar being

Empire Day celebrations at Wheatley Street School, before the First World War. The first Empire Day was in 1902. Schoolchildren sang patriotic songs, saluted the flag and were reminded of the greatness of the British Empire. *Courtesy of David Fry*

'especially intelligent' in the fourth to sixth standards. By 1901 the results of inspection visits to the school were 'entirely satisfactory'.

The old emphasis on domestic subjects for girls continued at the new Board schools and by 1878, Domestic Economy had become compulsory for girls. Classrooms at South Street were adapted in 1898 so that cookery classes could be started and later, Wheatley Street had a furnished flat where, recalled Mrs Rollaston, girls went for a month, to learn how to do things 'properly', namely household tasks such as laundry and sewing. As the years went on, there was little change in this emphasis and Mrs Lee remembered that when her sisters were learning how to do laundry at school, they were allowed to take in items for washing, particularly if there were difficulties, such as illness,

Teaching staff at Wheatley Street School in the 1890s. *Courtesy of David Fry*

at home. Another woman remembered being asked to take some socks into school that needed darning. They were her father's, with a huge hole at the bottom, only fit to be thrown away but she was terrified of the teacher because her work went all lumpy.

A Coventry school girl's 1942 domestic economy exercise book bears a striking resemblance to the work of Rosa Atkins at Blue Coat, back in 1873; it includes lessons on U bends, cleaning and washing glass, steel and iron brushes and how to clean a rug – shake it, vacuum or beat it with a stick, wash it with carpet soap, rub off the soap with a damp cloth and hang it out to dry and to not allow people to walk on it while it is wet.

Secondary Education for Girls

For working-class girls dreaming of pursuing a formal education in the early twentieth century, there were few ways in which this was possible beyond the age of 14 unless they attended a two-year training course to become pupil teachers or won a year's free place to attend evening classes at one of the Continuation Schools, which were attached to some of the city's elementary schools. At these, although it was possible to carry on with English and Mathematics and a few other subjects, the emphasis for girls remained on domestic skills, including needlework, dressmaking, housewifery, millinery, cookery and nursing.

In addition, the 1902 Education Act encouraged local education authorities to develop secondary schools' provision and in Coventry scholarship places were made available for boys who passed the selective examination at the two all-boys endowed grammar schools, Bablake and King Henry VIII. In 1907 Coventry City Council bought Barr's Hill, the former house of cycle manufacturer J.K. Starley for £5,500, and in 1908 it opened as the city's first secondary school for girls aged between 11 and (eventually) 18, offering free places to those pupils who passed the selective examination and fee paying places for the rest. In 1919 Barr's Hill was joined by the new Stoke Park Secondary School for Girls. Together these two schools opened up new opportunities for those girls able to take up their places. They could begin to take advantage of a world of higher education, of new training and jobs that had previously been closed to them. The first pupils to attend Barr's Hill were transferred from the city's Pupil Teacher Centre, dividing their time between Barr's Hill and teaching in schools across the city. The girls were prepared for the public academic examinations run by Cambridge University to denote national standards and Barr's Hill's first headmistress, Miss Grace Howell, 'did not rest until the advanced courses were introduced into the school and a strong sixth form sent many students annually to colleges and universities'. In addition a range of vocational studies such as typing and shorthand were offered to ensure that those girls who did not go on to higher education were able to find the sort of 'respectable' employment that parents were so keen for their daughters to move into.

Barr's Hill Girls' School, opened 1908. *Courtesy of David Fry*

The importance of girls' education was emphasised by Emily Penrose, Principal of Somerville College, Oxford, who in her speech at the opening of Barr's Hill, imagined with what interest and curiosity the city forefathers would look upon,

> These twentieth century maidens, for whom this time and treasure are being lavished, and if they asked why their fellow townsmen of the twentieth century have shown their patriotism in this way they would learn that it was that nowadays they have come to realise the serious importance to the nation of the best possible education of girls as of boys.

In their headmistress, the first girls had an excellent role model. Grace Howell was a graduate of the University of London which began to award degrees to women in the last quarter of the nineteenth century. This was in stark contrast to Oxford and Cambridge, where women were admitted to the women's colleges but not granted degrees (Oxford gave degrees to women for the first time in 1920 and Cambridge in 1948). Miss Howell was part of a generation of women that had fought hard for access to an education that was every bit as rigorous and challenging as that received by men. She was also no doubt familiar with widely expressed contemporary concerns that too much education was bad for young women's health. Some doctors claimed that if women tried to take on the level of study undertaken by men, their menstrual cycles would be adversely affected and as a result of too much energy being diverted to the brain, they may not be able to bear children. Despite research that proved this to be patently untrue, anxieties about girls' education remained.

At Barr's Hill's prize-giving ceremony in 1915, Sir Edward Manville, Chairman of the Daimler Motor Company, noted the phenomenal progress made by the school and said that the education of boys and girls was 'perhaps the most essential thing, as it was this which [would] enable the country to fight the world, not as we are fighting now, but mentally, and to keep our efficiency on the highest level'. But, as if to reassure his audience in the troubled times of war, he added that, 'All this education should not be at the expense of womanliness. It [is] desirable that all girls should grow up in the spirit of womanliness, as it [is] by the balance of womanliness and education that they [hope] to get the perfect woman.'

This was greeted with applause. A year earlier, Selina Dix, headmistress of Wheatley Street Girls' Elementary School had told a county meeting of the National Union of Teachers that,

> While all that is inherited in [woman] makes the home life peculiarly dependent on her, education has enlarged her view and the narrowness of the path trodden by the women of the early nineteenth century has broadened into a road which women and men may now tread together as equals in their work for the good of the world.

Grace Augusta Howell (1868-1940) was Barr's Hill's first headmistress and remained at the school until her retirement in 1932. Barr's Hill School Magazine, *Vita Nuova. Courtesy of Coventry History Centre*

As well as swotting for exams – and leaving to train to be teachers, doctors, pharmacists, nurses, librarians, musicians, artists and stage designers – the girls of both secondary schools were encouraged to get involved in charitable works, raising funds for local and national causes, including, (at Barr's Hill) collecting money to buy a dog called Basil for the Shackleton Antarctic Expedition in 1914 and making toys to send to poor children in Birmingham. During the Depression of the 1930s, Stoke Park's Charity representative sent a parcel of books and clothes to County Durham, reminding all that 'the distressed areas are still with us and will be in need of our help for a long time to come'.

One can imagine the excitement and pride with which new school uniform was purchased and worn by these first secondary school girls in Coventry. In 1912 the Barr's Hill uniform, approved by the Education Committee, included a school hat with hat band, a drill tunic of navy blue serge, India-rubber soled shoes for Drill and Games, a black linen overall for all scientific work, a white pinafore and cooking sleeves (for

The Art Room, Barr's Hill School. *Courtesy of David Fry*

housewifery students only) and it also advised that 'each girl should be provided with a mackintosh and umbrella'.

Of those pupils at Barr's Hill in 1911, the highest number of free places went to the daughters of artisans (skilled workers) and the highest number of fee-paying places to the daughters of merchants and manufacturers, with fees of up to £2 a year for Coventry residents and £2 13*s* for those living outside the city. Compared with the cost of sending a girl to one of the private schools available to middle-class girls, this was a very modest amount but nonetheless, it was beyond the means of many parents, and there were girls who, however much they wished to go on to secondary school, were unable to do so. One of the first girls to pass the exam for Stoke Park remembered her father taking her into the front room when the letter came and telling her that much as he would love her to go, how could she? There was uniform and books to buy and an expectation that she would stay on until she was 16. She was not upset or hurt by her father's decision because she knew that there was no

The Clock Room, Barr's Hill. *Courtesy of David Fry*

A sports lesson at Barr's Hill. *Courtesy of David Fry*

alternative and she did not want to make life any more difficult for him. When the Headmistress explained that there was a charity that would provide uniform, her mother, who had been a 'charity child', complete with shaved head, was mortified.

Boarding at Blue Coat in the 1930s, Ivy Hyland recalled her delight in learning that she had passed the scholarship exams for Barr's Hill. Keen to learn languages and 'good cookery', her dreams were dispelled by the Blue Coat Matron who told her that she would not be sent there but to Wheatley Street Elementary Girls' School, presumably because this was seen as education enough for a 'charity girl' being taught how to earn a living at the earliest possible age. Mrs Bucknell, at school in the 1920s, probably spoke for many girls when describing herself as a good scholar – too good for her own good in fact, she reckoned, because her family couldn't afford for her to continue in school after the age of 14. Instead she went into an elastic making factory, where the working day came as a big shock after school days.

Others were able to take up their places at the secondary schools but, because of the need to earn a living, could not progress to higher education or additional training, instead leaving at 16 to get a job and take qualifications at evening classes. The father who couldn't afford to send his daughter to Stoke Park in 1919 made sure that from the age of 12, she learned shorthand and typing so that she had the option of going into an office at 14, in his mind better than going onto the factory floor. Despite one girl's ambition to become a teacher, she was unable to stay on and instead her name was put down to work for the City Council, although she worked at Bushell's box making factory in Cow Lane in the meantime, attending night school three times a week. There were Council classes and private commercial colleges offering day and evening classes in shorthand, typing, business methods, English and correspondence. In the 1920s, the Coventry and District Co-operative Society and the Workers' Educational Association came together to plan programmes in Political Economy, Civics and Industrial History for a yearly fee of

2*s* 6*d*. The Co-op urged attendance at classes and study circles and warned that young people would regret it if they did not take up opportunities for adult education ('so often the university of the working man') and instead gave in to the current craze for pictures, whist and dancing. Laudable sentiments, but many 14 year olds, catapulted out of the classroom and into long hours in the workplace, needed either to sleep or to play at the end of the day, and it might be some years before they considered any return to further education. For many girls, of course, this was made almost impossible by marriage and motherhood and we will return to this in later chapters.

Learning in Wartime

Not long after the outbreak of the First World War, Coventry's Education Committee wrote to schools to encourage them to teach children about the causes of the war. At South Street Girls' School a series of pamphlets arrived, including one called 'Why Britain is at War' and teachers were asked to base their History and Geography lessons on these. Winter coal shortages meant that it was not always possible to have fires in school, and the girls were told to keep their jackets on, with temperatures in the classrooms and hall reaching just four degrees centigrade. Across the city, girls knitted socks for the troops, made sandbags and grenade bags, collected candles for the trenches, raised money for the YMCA, for hospitals, homes for disabled soldiers and brought in groceries for the Belgian refugees who had come to the city. At Barr's Hill there were garden parties to raise money for wounded soldiers in Coventry and Warwickshire Hospital and at Hill Crest Auxiliary Hospital, which opened next door to the school in 1915. Coventry's mayor, Mr Pridmore, told pupils and parents at Barr's Hill prize giving in 1915 that he had no doubt that girls passing out of school would do their duty to help their country in the present crisis and during the course of the war, the school magazine, *Vita Nuova*, listed the names of former pupils nursing in military hospitals at home and in France. Fear of German Zeppelin raids led to school air raid

Wheatley Street girls, collecting for Red Cross Day 1916. *Courtesy of Coventry History Centre*

drills and at South Street, girls practised drill by getting onto the floor and sitting under their desks because it was thought that if there was a raid during school hours, it would be safer to keep the girls at school than to send them home. When the Armistice was signed on 11 November 1918, children were given a long playtime, before being gathered to sing the National Anthem, salute the flag and cheer for the King, country and soldiers. Schools were then closed for the afternoon and the following day, giving teachers the chance to go home and join their families for celebrations.

Despite fuel and food shortages, there was far less disruption in school life during the First World War than in the Second (although at Barr's Hill, it was thought prudent to disband the German Club and turn it into a knitting circle). From 1939 problems for schools came thick and fast; there were evacuations, schools used as rest and first aid centres and the loss of over 4,000 school places as a result of air raids, in addition to over 1,200 lost because of the need to build shelters on school grounds. At Stoke Park School, trenches lined with benches were built into the lawns where lessons were meant to continue when air raid warnings had sounded, and at Barr's Hill the house basement was used as the shelter. Although classes continued at both schools, some pupils were evacuated to nearby towns including Leamington and Atherstone.

At Stoke Park, as in schools and households all over Britain, Victory in Europe was greeted with tremendous excitement:

> It was as though a spring had been contracted and let loose. Days beforehand the wireless had been switched on at dinner time and everyone had waited, listening for one word. Then, On May 7th, at 8 o clock, it came. Flags, bunting and coloured fairy lights appeared, bands played.

1945 and Beyond

The priority for Coventry City Council after the Second World War was to make sure that its increasing primary school population was accommodated in every way conceivable and affordable. Where possible damage was repaired, huts, halls and hostels were used until the building of new schools could begin. The 1944 Education Act divided schooling into primary and secondary units, which meant that secondary schooling was freely available to all, from the age of 11 until the new school leaving age of 15. The two girls' selective secondary schools remained and in 1945, were joined, on a temporary basis by Priory High School for Girls, the renamed senior section of Wheatley Street School and in 1953 by Coundon Court Girls' School.

As our period closes, academic opportunities for Coventry girls (and boys) were certainly greater than they had been a hundred years earlier but many of the old divisions – particularly those based on class and gender – remained. The 1944 Act also ushered in the eleven–plus exam and for those who passed, there was a better chance of receiving academic as opposed to vocational training. Interestingly, when the exam was introduced, it was ensured that the pass mark was lower for boys than for girls, because of fears that more girls than boys would qualify for places in selective schools. Attitudes towards girls' education were changing slowly but there were still many parents and employers wary of 'over-educating' young women who, after a few years, were still expected to place husband and family before career and find all their fulfilment in the making of home.

Girls from Priory High School (formerly the senior years of Wheatley Street School) at Stoke Branch Library, 1948. *Courtesy of Coventry History Centre*

CHAPTER TWO

Making a Living

Work represents so many things to women. Over the century, some women strove to be allowed to do paid work and to gain admission to professions regarded as male only domains. Others worked to feed themselves and their families. For some, work was companionable, opened new doors and was a refuge from domestic chores at home. There was pride in one's work, a sense of purpose and of belonging. For others it was relentless, oppressive and exhausting. For women with children, life could be horribly complicated; there were worries over childcare, childhood illnesses, shopping, cooking and running the house. In my own working life, all the above have applied at one time or another. I've taken jobs to fit in around my family. I've experienced guilt over hours worked (or not worked) and time spent away from the children, but there has been pleasure at jobs well done, at promotions and in friendships made. All of this helps me to understand something of the complications as well as the satisfactions of women's past paid and unpaid work.

Two Coventry women posing at a photographer's studio. The date is unknown but the styles of dress suggests it was taken in either the 1860s or 1870s. *Courtesy of the Herbert Art Gallery & Museum, Coventry*

Before the First World War

In Victorian Britain, women were expected to support their husbands in all their endeavours. While men went out to earn their living in the public world, their wives organised the household, provided their children with a robust moral code, looked attractive and offered comfort at the end of the long working day. A non-working wife was proof of a man's prestigious social standing, respectability and economic prowess. In return, the private sphere of the home was her domain and within this, she was protected from the harsh realities of business and politics by her husband. In the 1857 words of Coventry's very own philosopher, Charles Bray,

> If she feed us, clothe us, bring us into the world, educate us, nurse us, and make a home what it ought to be, this is her work; and if it is done properly, surely she will have enough to do – it is at least one-half of the business of life.

At least, this was the ideal. Whatever their station in life, all women's lives were affected by the widely held belief that marriage and motherhood were their ultimate goals, with no need for paid work. The reality of course was very different. Hundreds of thousands of women had no choice but to earn their own living or supplement the wages of their husbands and fathers and, because of the prevalent notion that their working lives would be short, after which they would be economically dependent on husbands, employers felt justified in paying them low wages. Men, on the other hand, were paid a higher 'family wage', in recognition of their duty towards wife and children – and regardless of whether they were married or single.

Social commentators like Bray believed that if a woman did need to earn a living, she should be engaged on work that was 'suitable' for the female sex, in other words, nothing which might lead to the contamination of her womanly virtues and nothing which would put her in direct competition with men. If she was engaged to cook, sew, launder, clean, serve, nurse, care or teach, then such work could go unchallenged – and to a large extent unnoticed – but if she moved into spheres of work that were traditionally claimed by men, then a great number of people had a great deal to say.

Nineteenth-century Factory work

Ribbon Weaving

By 1851, ribbon weaving, Coventry's largest industry, employed more women than men. Of a total population of 36,812, there were 10,641 people working in the production of the fancy silk ribbons that trimmed the nation's dresses, bonnets, shawls and children's clothing. The fact that about two thirds of those in the industry were women should not, however, fool us into thinking that this was an industry controlled or organised by women. By virtue of the apprenticeship, weaving was regarded as a skilled male occupation and was protected with pride by the men who had traditionally bought or rented their own looms and worked at home as 'outdoor' weavers, those who could afford to do so in the 'top shop' houses so characteristic of Coventry's craft background.

Many of these artisans married women who could ably assist them at the loom, women who came to know the craft as well as their husbands, teaching their children to help out in the family business whenever needed. The autobiography of Coventry weaver Joseph Gutteridge (1816–99) illustrates some of the ways in which families lived and worked through hard times. His second wife, Mary, was not only 'well versed in weaving' but also 'thrifty in household management'. Gutteridge praised her 'patient and plodding endurance' which helped them to survive some very lean times in an industry prone to major depressions.

Coventry craftsmen despised the inevitable arrival of factory production despite the fact that it was sometimes possible to earn higher and steadier wages there than in the home workshop. Young, single women might have preferred the relative independence of working outside the home but for married women, life in the factory could be unbearably tough. Traditionally, weaving families had the flexibility to set their

Top shops in the 'weavers' suburb' of Hillfields, where those who could afford to do so moved to escape the cramped conditions of the city centre. The large windows front and back provided the best light for weaving. In order to protect the family from the noise of the loom, rags were often packed under the topshop floor and the bedroom ceilings underneath. *Courtesy of Coventry History Centre*

own working hours, which was at least a little compensation for the constant anxiety caused by the instability in the trade. They could work extremely long days but then, as long as the work was completed on time, they might have Sunday and 'St Monday' free before starting up again on Tuesday. Such Mondays, while an opportunity for leisure for the husband, were, in all probability, used by his wife to do the laundry and catch up with other household chores. Nonetheless, this lifestyle provided the chance to keep an eye on the children as opposed to the factory women, witnessed by the Medical Officer of Health,

> at an early hour ... on their way to the mills, with their children only half-dressed, carrying the remainder of their clothes and their food for the day, to be left with the person who has charge of the child during its mother's absence, and this oft-times on a cold winter's morning in the midst of sleet or snow.

The pathos apparent in this 1856 'observation' reveals a wider concern about women factory workers in a city that was as yet far from used to their presence. Charles Bray thought that factory working made young girls too independent, especially those from the countryside, living away from their parents and liable to fall into 'bad company' and lose 'all natural modesty' due to the 'indiscriminate mixing of the sexes' in factories. Not only that, but such employment would, he was sure, lead to the early marriages of couples with no savings and wives with 'no knowledge of housekeeping, and none of the duties of maternity'. This, he felt sure, would lead inevitably to 'a fearful infant mortality' because of the practice of leaving children to go to work.

Watchmaking

Coventry's other important industry for much of the nineteenth century was watchmaking. As in ribbon weaving, here there was a great deal of male craft pride and it was not until towards the end of the century that women were employed in any significant numbers, as production began to shift from small workshops into larger units and factories turning out cheaper goods made in less time. In 1852, Charles Dickens, on a visit to Rotherham's Watch Factory in Spon Street, had predicted that in time the men would not be able to continue to keep the women out of a trade in which,

> No work can be more suitable for women. The fineness of sight and touch required seems to mark it out as a feminine employment; and it can be pursued at home, if that is desired, just like needlework.

Yet, according to Charles Bray, not only were men opposed to women in the watch trade 'because they know it means more work and less wages', but because they regarded themselves as respectable artisans who were,

> Provident in their habits – do not marry early, keep their wives at home, send their children to school till the age of fourteen, belong to Building Societies, Freehold Land Societies and Sick Clubs and are generally well conducted.

In other words, their wives and daughters might usefully help out in the trade as long as it was more or less done behind closed doors to keep up the illusion of men being solely responsible for keeping their families.

Three women holding their own in a male dominated workshop environment in the early 20th century. John Dutson's factory in Trafalgar Street made electroplated parts for the watch industry. *Courtesy of David Fry*

Women workers in greater numbers, at Williamson's Watch and Clock Factory in the early twentieth century. *Courtesy of David Fry*

Amy Hurlston, daughter of a Spon End watch manufacturer, observed that the majority of those women who were engaged in watchmaking were unmarried, because the household duties that married women had to attend to roughened their hands and made them unfit for the fine work required. Amy, born in 1865, grew up watching and learning the trade, no doubt helping out within the family, yet she does not seem to have earned an independent living from the industry. Instead, by the time she was in her twenties, she was pursuing the sort of unpaid work more familiar to that of a daughter from a middle-class family, including becoming one of Coventry's first women Poor Law Guardians. Unusually for a working class young woman, her income was derived from her success as a journalist and as the author of popular or 'sensational' novels, such as *The Memorials of the Dead in St Michael's Church, Coventry* and *Played Out and Lost*, both published in 1885. In 1896 she left Coventry to take up the post of Lady Editor of the *Sheffield Weekly Telegraph*.

A New Century, a New Coventry?

By the start of the twentieth century, both the ribbon and watch industries had lost their prominence. A catastrophic crash in the silk industry in 1860, caused by the removal of import duties on continental ribbons, led, according to Gutteridge, to unprecedented poverty levels in Coventry. Many families emigrated and, as soon as it became possible, workers moved into new opportunities, leaving the ribbon trade in the hands of a few men overseeing a predominantly female workforce. While the weaving trade continued to decline, with the exception of specialist firms such as Cash's in Foleshill and Thomas Stevens in Cox Street, the textile tradition among Coventry

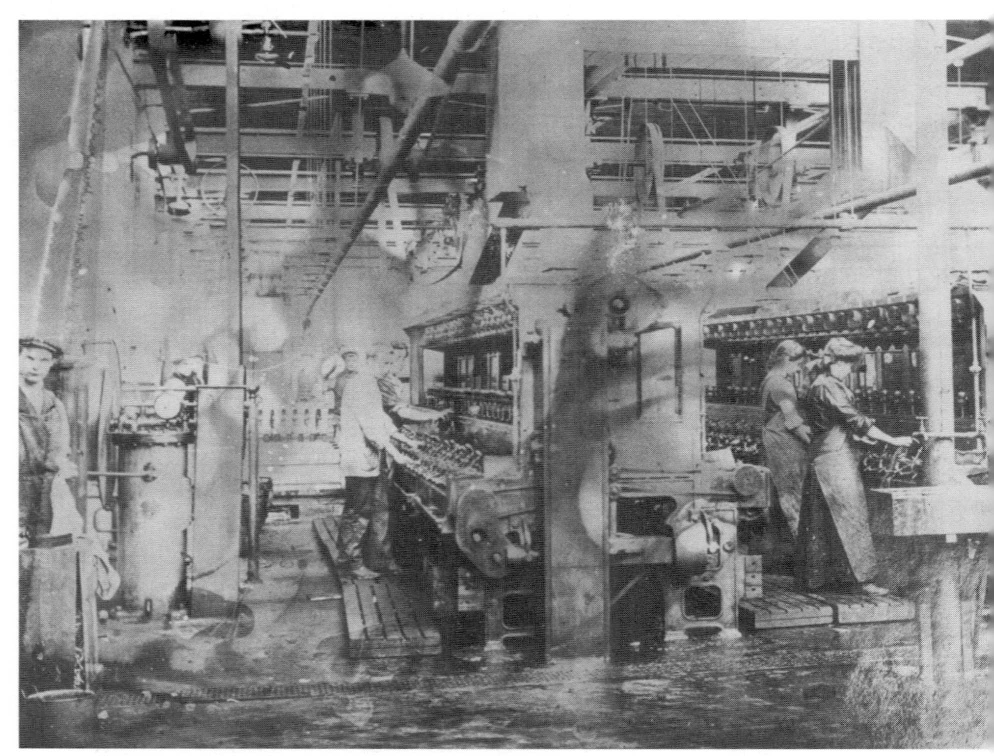

Workers at Courtaulds, Foleshill Road, before the First World War, standing on platforms to keep their feet and clothes dry. *Courtesy of the Herbert Art Gallery & Museum, Coventry*

Courtaulds' workers outside the Foleshill Road factory. *Courtesy of David Fry*

women workers continued, with the opening of Leigh Mills in Hill Street in 1863, for woollen goods, intended to provide employment for former ribbon workers, and then, in 1904, with Courtaulds' rayon factory on Foleshill Road, which employed over 800 women by 1907.

In watchmaking, most of the small, home-based firms had disappeared, leaving factories such as Williamson's on Holyhead Road and Rotherham's and the Coventry Movement Company, in Spon Street. In 1911 the factories employed a few hundred women and just over a thousand men.

By the start of the twentieth century, new economic ventures had taken hold in the city. The birth of the motor industry in Coventry is a much-told tale of a meteoric rise and by 1911 nearly 13,000 people were employed within it. A chain of events led to its take off, from the establishment of the Coventry Sewing Machine Company in 1863, through diversification into cycle production in the 1870s and the attraction of capital into the production of motor vehicles from the 1890s. From the start, these were male dominated industries but the introduction of small numbers of female workers was viewed with deep suspicion, largely because employers paid women less than the men who feared that their own wages would be dragged down as a result.

Work in the cycle trades could be dirty and unhealthy and some men used this to explain why they thought women should be removed from the factories. In 1908, the Brassworkers' Union distributed a leaflet urging parents and friends of women working as cycle polishers to see that this work would damage health and shorten lives, and that women would earn no more money than they would get in a cleaner, healthier trade. Others sounded like Charles Bray in the 1850s, one clergyman declaring that 'a bicycle shop was no proper place for a woman to be employed in at all'. Too many workshops, he wrote, had terrible and degrading atmospheres and young girls were exposed to the coarsening effects of 'language as would not be tolerated for a moment in an honest working man's home'. Both church and male trade unionists believed that woman's dignity was best preserved by keeping her out of the cycle factories where her employment was a 'standing disgrace', preventing women from taking up 'their natural and ideal positions as the helpmates and partners of men in every sense of the word' and becoming 'what God intended her to be – the noblest influence for good upon earth'.

Domestic Service

Yet women worked where they could, for what wages they could get and there were few public objections to the hard physical work that was traditionally seen as rightfully belonging to women. Having a smaller middle class than some towns and cities, there were proportionately fewer female domestic servants in Coventry than in some more affluent places but nevertheless nearly a fifth of women worked as servants, cleaners or caterers in private households, pubs, hotels and laundries in and around the city.

The most common experience for a Coventry servant was in a moderately sized household where the mistress might employ a cook and a housemaid or – worst of all for a young girl – just one maid of all work, where conditions depended entirely on the kindness – or otherwise – of the employer. Hours of work were longer even than in the factory, typically extending from six in the morning to ten at night, but hidden away in the private world of the home, very few people raised concerns about women's involvement in this type of arduous, heavy and often dirty work.

Rosa Atkins, the Blue Coat girl we met in Chapter One, knew in theory what lay ahead of her when she moved into service but little can have prepared her for the exhaustion felt at filling her entire day – for up to six and a half days a week – 'doing' for the family, taking care to be neatly dressed, grabbing meals when she could and accepting that there was always something to be done, from mending clothes to polishing the silver. An advertisement for a live-in general servant who 'must be fond of children' might sound alarm bells for a more experienced girl who would understand that she was also needed to take on babysitting duties, perhaps during her evenings 'off' when mistresses would argue that the servant was there anyway and may as well be taken advantage of. Wages were low and justified on the basis that board and lodgings were provided.

Just as girls from the so-called 'industrial schools' were found employment as servants, so girls were regularly removed from the workhouse into service; in 1889, 13-year-old Elizabeth Moorcroft was 'allowed' to go into service with Thomas Gosling, a market gardener who agreed to pay her a fairly typical one and a half shillings a week along with board and lodging, washing and any necessary medical attendance, as long as the workhouse kitted her out with two complete sets of clothes. If girls were met with kindness, this could be a little compensation for being separated from their families, who might remain in the workhouse.

This was not the case for 11-year-old Lucy Sly who was taken out of the workhouse in 1888 to work as a servant in

W. Turrall, grocer's shop on Harnall Lane at the start of the twentieth century. On the right is an advertisement for American singer Madame Alice Esty, performing at the Empire Theatre. *Courtesy of Coventry History Centre*

Foleshill. At a court hearing at which her mistress was fined 10*s* for striking her, it was alleged that Lucy's ill treatment included being kept up until two in the morning to do the washing up and being denied food. The court ruled that her mistress had no doubt been provoked by the child's untidy habits but that she had been corrected with unnecessary severity. When Lucy was returned to the workhouse, she did so with many cuts and bruises. The case against her master who had allegedly thrown a boot at her, striking her in the eye, was dismissed. The future for girls like Lucy Sly was uncertain, to say the very least.

Despite the low wages and long hours, some families believed that domestic service carried with it more prestige than factory work and one Coventry woman believed that her aunts looked down on her mother who, as just 'a factory girl', had never learned, as they had, to correctly and smartly set the table at big family occasions. Others, however, recognised merely the sheer drudgery of the work. May Purnell's mother, a domestic at Coventry and Warwickshire Hospital in the first years of the twentieth century, scrubbed corridors, did the laundry and 'whatever she was asked to do'. By the time she came home to her family of six, 'she was dead beat', after a day literally spent on her hands and knees. If there were any perks to the job, it was that the cook used to secretly parcel up leftovers from the tables – bread and butter and rock cakes – to take home for the children – 'and we were glad of it'.

Serving the Community

Domestic and textile work might have been the largest categories of female work in the pre-First World War years but then, as now, women turned their hands to a whole range of occupations. One woman, born in 1892, recalled how, after her father died, her mother had to go out 'scrubbing and washing and everything else' to support her six children. Times were hard but thanks to her mother's resourcefulness, the family owed nothing to anyone and ate 'the best' of food. Although it was not customary – and certainly not regarded as respectable – for women to drink in

The manageress (seated) of the Hare and Hounds pub on Gulson Road. Between 1911 and 12 the pub was an all-female concern, run by Mrs Clara Tully who lived there with barmaids Anne Cutler and Maud Harris, with general servant Sarah Randle. *Courtesy of Albert Smith*

public, it was not uncommon to find landladies ruling inns and taverns with a rod of iron, accepted because, despite nominally belonging to the male dominated and public world of business, they were – along with their poorly paid barmaids – in essence still carrying out a very traditional female role – serving men with food and drink.

Women also served in shops and markets, as assistants, managers and owners. When Sarah Goode was widowed in 1878, she placed a notice in the paper to earnestly solicit a share of the patronage and support of friends and the ladies of Coventry and vicinity in her new business at number seven, the Burges. She described the business, to be run with her daughter, as a Millinery and Fancy Repository, selling 'a choice and varied assortment of Bonnets, Hats, Flowers, Feathers, Ribbons, Laces, Velvets, Hosiery, Gloves, Haberdashery etc'. It may sound genteel but it was a question of how to survive in a world without widows' and old age pensions. Mrs Goode was just 51 and her daughter 25 and the value of the estate left to them was £800, enough to buy the business but not sufficient to guarantee them a secure future.

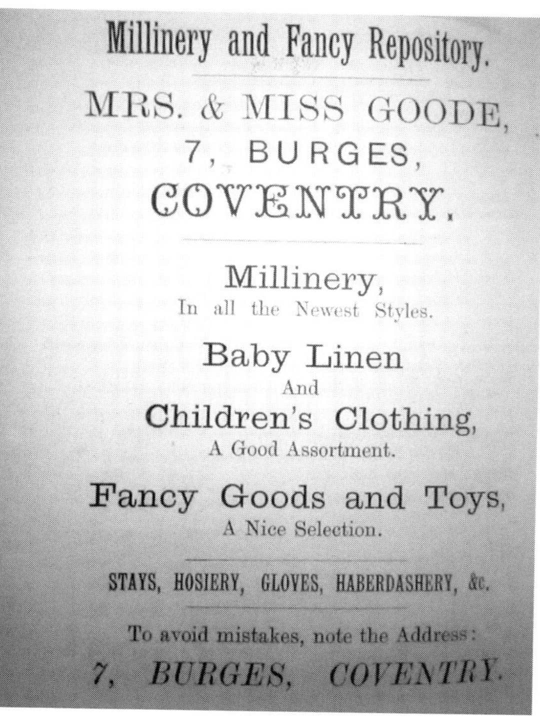

Advertisement for Mrs & Miss Goode's Millinery and Fancy Repository, 1879, *Coventry Directory. Courtesy of Coventry History Centre*

Before the First World War, women who taught or nursed might be well thought of within their local community but both fields of work were slow to gain professional status, again largely because these occupations were seen as typically suited to a woman's nature and as such merely an extension of her natural caring role. Even after reformers had done a great deal to turn nursing into a respected field, low pay was justified by the notion that women should be motivated to nurse not by money but by a desire to care for people. At the start of the twentieth century, by no means all who worked as nurses had received formal training and they worked in many different capacities, from caring for individual patients in a household to working in a workhouse infirmary, hospital or asylum. Similarly, many nineteenth-century midwives were technically untrained but they learned instead from older, more experienced women and performed crucial, affordable services for working-class women giving birth at home. The majority of women could not afford to be attended by a doctor and often, the midwife would provide much more than medical care, taking on domestic chores and some childcare until the mother

Women working at Boots' Cash Chemists, Broadgate, before the First World War. *Courtesy of the Herbert Art Gallery & Museum, Coventry*

was back on her feet again, and offering what all new mothers need – reassurance and practical advice.

In the 1901 census, just thirteen women were identified as midwives in Coventry and just over a hundred as sick nurses and invalid attendants, but many more women came to the help of neighbours and friends. May Purnell remembered that her mother, despite being a single, working parent with six children of her own, would always be called on if any neighbours were ill or in trouble. She would also help the local midwife by taking her bag and going on ahead of her, setting everything up for the confinement and laying out baby clothes in readiness. Similarly, Mrs Bucknell's mother did her best to help everyone, including laying people out at death.

For many working class women, the only way to receive teacher training was to become apprenticed to a school for five years, often between the ages of 13 and 18, working in the

Boots the Chemist's Broadgate store, 1911. *Courtesy of Pictures of Coventry*

classroom and receiving additional instruction from the head teacher. In April 1897, South Street School's log-book confirms that its pupil teachers took exams in arithmetic in the morning and then spent three hours in the evening on history and music papers. Two days later it was apparent to the headmistress that there had been great improvement in their history knowledge

Midwife Mrs Sarah Hannah Reid, of George Street. She was enrolled onto the Central Midwives' Board in 1912. *Courtesy of David Fry*

and she recommended that they should supplement their learning with some historical novels, including Dickens' *A Tale of Two Cities* and Walter Scott's *Heart of Midlothian.* In 1879 Mrs Scrivens went to see the head teacher at Spon Gate School, anxious because her daughter Florrie's teaching apprenticeship was about to expire. The family could not afford the next step, which was to attend college and so she hoped that the school might keep her on to work as an uncertificated teacher. The opening of the pupil teacher centre at Wheatley Street School around 1900 helped many girls to earn and train at the same time but it was not until after the First World War that more working class girls, such as Margery Evans, were able to go away from home to training college. Margery was born in 1907 and attended Barr's Hill Secondary School for Girls. Having decided to become a teacher, she went to the Home and Colonial College in London, the cost eased by the award of maintenance grants from two Coventry charities.

Teachers at Stoke National School in the early twentieth century. *Courtesy of the Herbert Art Gallery & Museum, Coventry*

Times were hard, jobs were tough but women workers stood up for themselves, fighting injustices when and where they could, displaying courage by confronting bosses who imagined that women would accept work conditions and pay without resistance. In the early twentieth century, some local women joined trade unions, although this was a very risky business, frowned upon by bosses who expected female employees to be accepting and docile, and those regarded as trouble makers could not merely lose their jobs but be blacklisted by other firms. A woman trade union organiser held an outdoor meeting in Coventry, only for the audience to flee when the manager of a nearby factory came by. It was not until the evening when a social gathering was held 'that we were able to hold the undivided attention of the girls' and encourage them to listen to the union message. Before the

The Coventry branch of the National Federation of Women Workers was formed in 1907. Here the women celebrate the end of a successful strike for improved pay and conditions at Messrs Cramp's blouse making factory, 1913. Standing on the far left is honorary organiser, Mrs Sarah Griffiths. Third from left on front row, Edith Mayell. *Courtesy of Mrs Enid Trent*

war there were two main trade unions for women industrial workers – the all-female National Federation of Women Workers and the mixed-sex Workers' Union. The Federation's local branch, started in 1907, was bolstered by two successful strikes in 1913, one at the Coventry Chain Company in Spon End, where the threat of wage deductions was lifted, and the other at Cramps' blouse-making firm in Much Park Street, where low piece rates were raised. National organisers were careful to protect young local activists, including Edith Mayell (nee Stringer), by keeping them from negotiations with employers who might victimise them at a later date.

The First World War

As men volunteered for, and were later conscripted into, the armed services, women answered the nation's call to supply munitions, to help run public services and transport and to nurse the wounded at home and abroad. Women were used to being adaptable, to turning their hands to anything demanded of them, so it was no surprise when they took on a wide range of jobs and duties during the First World War, many of which had been (and would be again) regarded as men's work. Women had a range of motives for taking on munitions work; Elsie Farlow left Leigh Mills to go to the Royal Ordnance Factory in Red Lane, wanting to feel as bold and grown up as the other girls who'd left weaving behind. There *were* higher wages to be earned, new jobs to be experienced, opportunities to move away from home and live less restricted lives than previously. Nationally, around 800,000 women moved into factory work during the war, many leaving behind the low pay and isolation of domestic service or low paid industrial labour. In 1915 the *Midland Daily Telegraph* noted that 'every day sees the extension of the employment of female labour in Coventry, and citizens are now becom-

A Coventry postwoman during the First World War. *Courtesy of David Fry*

ing accustomed to seeing women in positions that up to a few months ago were invariably filled by men'. Women were driving delivery vans; passengers on the city trams were 'amazed with the wonderful adaptability shown by the fair sex' as conductors and, thanks to the postwomen and girl telegraph messengers working for the Post Office, the Coventry Postmaster had been able to release five more men to join the Post Office Rifles.

Yet, not only were such extensions to women's work largely temporary, with expectations that they would return to more traditional roles the moment the war was over, many men, despite propaganda depicting women industrial workers as heroines, were not prepared to accept the arrival of thousands of women into engineering roles until their own long-term labour positions had been secured. For many women, it became possible to earn more than they had ever done before but few received equal pay with men. The more normal position in

White and Poppe's National Filling Factory, Holbrooks, 1916. By the end of this year, there were 4000 women and 800 men employed at this factory. *Courtesy of David Fry*

munitions factories was for a 'dilution' of processes whereby several unskilled workers did the work of one skilled man, thus justifying lower pay and preserving the status of the craftsman when he returned to industry after the war. In addition, much of the work was exhausting, and where wages were high, much of this was due to the long hours worked and excessive overtime that was not always voluntary.

The war transformed Coventry into one of the country's most important munitions centres, with its engineering firms swiftly converting production to military equipment. In 1916 a government report stated that 'Coventry now presents in miniature some of the features of an American town, an agglomeration of girls and women, English, Scotch, Irish and Welsh, having been thrown together for war work'. Between January and mid-October 1916 alone, 5,000 women came to work in Coventry. Many more workers 'pour daily in and out of Coventry' on packed trains; it was not uncommon to see women fainting in the morning and evening crushes caused by the overlap of shift workers. Once at work, despite increasing safety measures implemented as the war progressed, there were some appalling accidents on the factory floor. Florence Jackson recalled that at the Coventry Ordnance Fuse Factory, women 'used to fill the shell bodies with powder, and often one blew up ... occasionally you'd get a spark off and it will go ... my stepmother worked there. One of her friends, they said had her face blown to bits'. In 1917 Ada Curtis, a young woman from Kettering lodging in Earlsdon, was killed instantly in a local factory and in 1918 24-year-old Florence Johnson died when detonators exploded as they fell from the tray she was carrying. At the end of the war, several Coventry women, including Annie Brown, Agnes Ferguson, Elizabeth Fletcher, Elsie White and Alice Brown, were awarded OBEs for courage, high example and presence of mind shown during munitions factory fires and explosions.

There were other hazards; the painful and potentially fatal results of working with the chemical substances which were used to produce explosives and treat the wings of aircraft eventually led to the issuing of Ministry of Munitions rules for those working with TNT. These included the presence of medical officials in the factories, the provision of protective clothing, 'approved fluids' for the cleaning of the skin, adequate ventilation and a free half pint of milk for every worker. The official line was that the work was safe as long as precautions were taken and workers did not get careless. The reality for the 'canary girls', whose skin was turned yellow by too much exposure to TNT, was that this was an unavoidable consequence of their work.

Women munitions workers may have been the nation's heroines but there was considerable moral panic at the idea of so many young women away from families and a strong desire at every possible opportunity to tell them how they should live their lives. The Ministry of Munitions employed women to protect workers in the factories but also to search them for potentially dangerous 'contraband' such as matches and

Women shell fillers at Hotchkiss and Cie's Gosford Street Factory, First World War. *Courtesy of David Fry*

cigarettes. In many parts of the country, anxieties about women war workers' social behaviour had also led to the establishment of women's voluntary patrol groups, to keep watch over young people in public places and try to ensure that the new freedoms of women living in hostel accommodation did not result in illicit encounters with young men, whose attentions should be firmly fixed on winning the war, not on larking about with loose women workers. In the spring of 1917 two women, Miss Glover and Miss Rendall, were appointed to Coventry City's Police Force and by 1918 there were four, out of a force of 141. The Council's Watch Committee, with responsibility for the city's police, decided to appoint women officers on a full time basis for the duration of the war only, with an expectation that their work would be largely preventive, that they would liaise with factory welfare workers to make sure that women workers were safe and behaving appropriately. Florence Glover, who came to Coventry from Bath as a wartime police constable, was, at 39,

Policewomen at Coventry railway station September 1917, as Queen Mary and the Princess Royal arrive to visit a munitions factory. *Courtesy of David Fry*

considerably older than many of the women she was watching over. I wonder what clashes there might have been between her and the spirited young women factory workers, who were not keen on someone telling them how to live their lives and assuming the worst of them, especially when this was dressed up as concern for their safety.

None of the policewomen were retained after the war and, despite appeals from city social workers for women police, it was not until 1938 that the City Council finally agreed to the appointment of two women, but even then, it was on the understanding that they would not be able to wear uniform. Just three years earlier, Alderman Wyles had stated that there was no justification for women strutting about the streets wearing leggings, short skirts, belts and helmets, making an exhibition of themselves! The National Council of Women (NCW), which campaigned persistently for the reintroduction of Coventry women police, was later able to report, 'with quiet satisfaction', that in 1957, Mrs Inspector Green of the Coventry City Police spoke to the NCW about the formation of the women's branch of the Force, which by then consisted of 2,250 officers nationwide.

Nursing

While by far the largest number of women war workers in Coventry were employed in industry, those who had less need for full time wages took up work as British Red Cross Voluntary Aid Detachment (VAD) nurses to support trained nursing staff in the care of wounded soldiers. By the end of the War, 90,000 women had served as VADs. Coventry and Warwickshire Hospital had been placed on war footing by the end of 1914, with 180 military beds and new wards added by 1916, by which time thirty-one VADs were on duty each day and night, drawn from the Warwick 70 Division, under Commandant Mrs A.E. Cramp and Quarter Master, Mrs Gertrude Beamish. In addition, there were two VAD hospitals, Hillcrest on the Radford Road and one housed in Courtaulds' gymnasium in Foleshill. In August

1916 the *Coventry Standard* carried an appeal from the British Red Cross for more VAD nurses, stating that 'there must still be many women who are not giving the whole of their time and service to the war and who have no ties which prevent them from doing so'. Convoys of wounded soldiers arrived from the ports in hospital trains and were greeted, transported and settled onto the military wards by VADs and orderlies. Olive Mary Reynolds who joined VAD 70 in 1917, was instructed by Commandant Cramp to report for duty at Coventry and Warwickshire Hospital after the arrival of one such convoy.

Being a VAD provided some women with the opportunity to travel; some went to military hospitals across the country and others went abroad. Althea Seymour, from Whitley, had joined the VADs in 1913 and, with valuable training already under her belt when she went to Hillcrest in early 1915, she went on to serve in Salonika, France and Egypt. Like other VADs, she was awarded service medals for her war work.

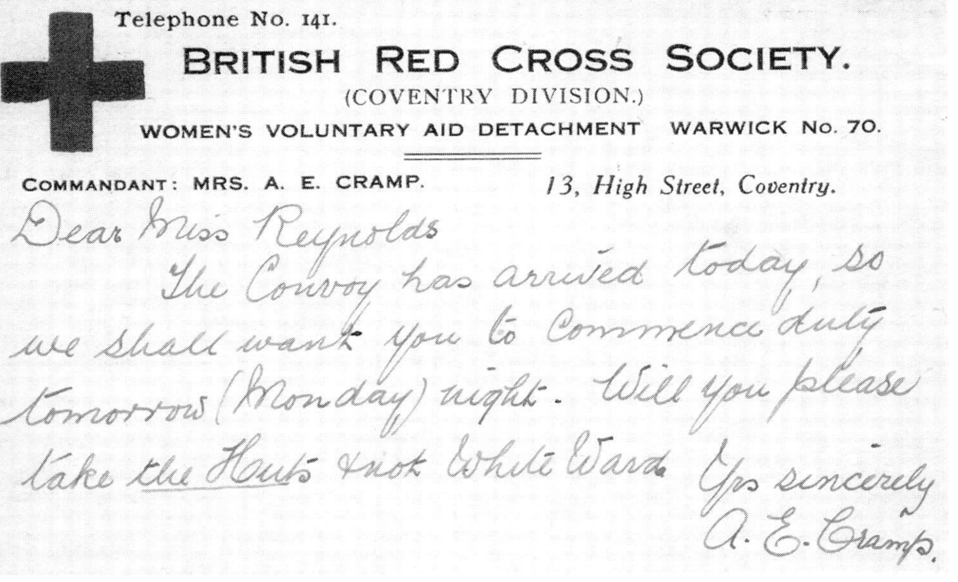

Telephone No. 141.

BRITISH RED CROSS SOCIETY.

(COVENTRY DIVISION.)

WOMEN'S VOLUNTARY AID DETACHMENT WARWICK No. 70.

COMMANDANT: MRS. A. E. CRAMP. 13, High Street, Coventry.

Dear Miss Reynolds

The Convoy has arrived today, so we shall want you to commence duty tomorrow (Monday) night. Will you please take the Huts & not White Ward. Yrs sincerely

A. E. Cramp.

Instruction sent to Miss Reynolds informing her of her duties with the Women's Voluntary Aid Detachment (VAD) during the First World War. *Courtesy of David Fry*

The services of trained and volunteer nurses did not go unnoticed by the government. Several Coventry nurses, including nursing sisters L and M Hirst at Coventry and Warwickshire and Miss Ratcliff (a masseuse), were commended to the Secretary of State for War. The VAD Commandant of Hillcrest was awarded an OBE and Mrs Cramp of VAD Warwick 70, an MBE. Miss A Selby was honoured for her two years' continuous night service.

By 1917 the Workhouse Infirmary at the top of London Road was recognised as a training school for midwifery and, as Coventry and Warwickshire Hospital filled up with wounded soldiers, doctors began sending more women to the Infirmary because they knew that there they would have a better chance to deliver babies safely under proper hygienic conditions. One woman who trained at the Workhouse Infirmary after the war acknowledged the thoroughness of the training offered, providing her with an excellent base from which to move forwards to gain midwifery experience and later to become a ward sister in another part of the country.

After the War

When the war ended, munitions factories closed down and engineering factories reverted to peacetime production. Many women left the city to go back to their home towns, such as the Ordnance worker given a free pass home to her native Belfast, having to leave behind her friend who was in Coventry and Warwickshire Hospital following an accident in a factory right at the end of the war. In Coventry, as in other former munitions centres, unemployment among women soared as men were demobilised and pre-war working conditions resumed. Some women were no doubt thankful to be able to give up paid work and focus on life in the home after the strains of war but a great many had no choice but to carry on earning, as single women, as wives, as mothers, as widows or as carers for disabled soldiers. In early 1919 there were so many unemployed women in the city that a special women's department of the Labour Exchange opened at the municipal baths in Priory Street. There wasn't much work to be had apart from domestic service, which, with its low wages was extremely unpopular, but women were warned that if they did not take suitable work, they would lose their out of work benefit.

With the writing on the wall, two Coventry women trade union organisers, Alice Arnold and Henrietta Givens, did all they could to try to raise the status of domestic service and encourage mistresses not to insist on hiring live-in servants, so that women did not merely disappear back into the isolation they had experienced before the war. They reported the case of one young woman who, before the war, had worked as an indoor parlour maid, earning £30 a year with a uniform provided. In 1919, having turned down a position at £28 without the provision of uniform, she lost her unemployment benefit. Their attempts, however, amounted to little (apart from some irritation from mistresses wondering why on earth women would want to live independently when they could have a perfectly nice room with their employer. Surely, said one, it was hardly conducive to decent morals to have women parading the streets at night when they could be safe in the household) and by 1931, more women in Coventry were employed in domestic service and domestic work than in any other employment sector. You took what you could get; a former Ordnance worker took a job at the Cosy Café in Hertford Street. Out of her first week's wages, paid in advance, she was required to buy two aprons, a plain lunchtime one with a bib and another for afternoon tea service, which was a little lacier.

A trade depression from 1921 led to a great deal of short time working, with one woman recalling the difficulties; 'I should think I worked for four firms that closed down – no sooner had you got a job and got settled in than the auditors came in' and it was back to square one. When Mrs Dingley worked at Fred Lee's jewel works in Dover Street, the pattern was, for some time, three days of work, followed by three off. Workers were given their employment cards to take to the Labour Exchange on Thursday and would be back at work by Monday, having received a small amount of benefit to cover the unemployed

Typists employed at the GEC, *The Loudspeaker,* January 1929. *Courtesy of Coventry History Centre*

days. As well as at the Labour Exchange, some women asked for work at the factory gate in the hope of getting lucky.

As before the war, a large number of women in Coventry worked in the textile industries. Courtaulds was regarded by parents as a superior and respectable establishment for young women to work in and appointment was often through the recommendation of family or friends. It paid more than most other sectors of the local textile industry and in addition, the factory had a reputation for strict shop-floor discipline, safety, segregation of the sexes and for keeping a close eye on girls' physical and moral wellbeing. Mrs Brown, who worked in reeling, remembered being watched all the time; the work was checked every hour and there would be questions if you hadn't done as much in that hour as a previous one.

Another popular choice and large employer of women was the General Electric Company (GEC) where wages, although not as high as Courtaulds, were still better than in many other industrial jobs available to women. Mrs Bucknell, for example, was employed at the Humber factory, polishing wooden car trimmings. It was, she thought, reasonable money but she did feel the injustice of earning less than the men. In 1921, the basic local rate for women in engineering firms was slashed by nearly 8*s* a week. Some firms found other ways to cut costs; one worker said that she had never been so indignant as when she was told that out of her 16*s* weekly pay, she had to buy her own glue for a shilling to carry out her work at Fred Lees' Dover Street factory.

'The Winners of the Race at Lunchtime': GEC women workers leaving work on the stroke of noon, *The Loudspeaker,* January 1926. *Courtesy of Coventry History Centre*

The number of women entering office and shop work in the inter-war period increased. Parents regarded both as decent, respectable work for their daughters. In the first chapter, we saw how a father tried to ease the blow of not being able to afford to send his daughter to Stoke Park School by paying for shorthand lessons to prepare her for office work. Others went into the factory but learned bookkeeping and secretarial skills at night school, having put their names down for local government work upon leaving school.

The assumption that women's working lives ended at marriage continued to ensure that they were paid less than men. In addition, some firms operated either a marriage bar, formally in the case of Courtaulds, less so in the case of other factories where there was an unspoken rule that a woman would leave as soon as she married. Things at the GEC were different; in 1929, the firm's magazine, *The Loudspeaker,* included in its short profiles of workers, Mrs Shaw, a shop clerk in Wireless Assembly and her husband, in the Model Room. It was hoped that they would remain at the firm for many more than the nine years they had already done. But let's not think for a moment that the GEC was promoting equality; an earlier article on the magazine's Ladies Page had reminded women of their need to have sufficient training to cope with 'real life' as wives, mothers and housewives. A man, it was reckoned, might 'be caught by the glance of a bright eye, by a pair of cherry cheeks, by a handsome figure' but, once the knot is tied, he finds out that his love cannot mend a shirt or cook a pudding. Then woe to the unhappy man and also to the unhappy woman, because then all becomes hateful and 'the public house separates those whom the Law and the Church have joined together'.

It was not just industry that operated the marriage bar. In the 1930s, Coventry City Council's women officers were required to resign upon marriage. The usual and often unspoken reason for such rulings was to ensure, during periods of economic depression, that an equality of income within households was maintained (the old assumption that married women had no need to work). As far back as 1908 the Education Committee had decided to terminate the contracts of all its married women teachers to ensure positions for all single women teachers seeking employment. In 1933 there was fresh concern about the forty-four married women teachers in the city. Councillor Emily Smith argued against the marriage bar, believing strongly that women must have the right to live their own lives as seemed best to them. Men, she said, all too readily arranged and decided what kind of life women should lead and although it might be argued that there was inequality in a man and his wife both bringing money into the house while the man next door was unemployed, she urged the men to see that the reality was much more complicated than this at first implied. If councillors received pay, she stated, she and her female colleagues would no longer be able to serve the city and in fact, it may as well be said to all women, whatever their occupation, 'Go back home and do the housework. This world has no use for you'.

Breaking Down Barriers

For many women, then, the inter war years were characterised by a continuation of work that was regarded as traditionally female, lower pay than men and assumptions that their working lives would be short, if not sweet. But there were breakthroughs; in 1919, the year after women over 30 received the right to vote in parliamentary elections, the Sex Disqualification (Removal) Act was passed, allowing women to progress through the ranks of professions from which they had previously been excluded, such as accountancy and the law. By 1919, women doctors had been practicing medicine since 1865 but they were few in number and opportunities to practice limited. In 1929, Dr Elsie Humpherson, who grew up in Coventry and qualified in 1913, addressed pupils at her alma mater, Warwick High School for Girls. Speaking of the opportunities for women medics that had arisen because of the war, she warned of the difficulties of entering a profession which, to a large extent, meant giving up one's life to the work. However, she also drew attention to the tremendous chances that existed for social service, emphasising the caring and human aspects of the work rather than personal ambition and career advancement. She had established her career as a medical officer in the welfare department of Birmingham's health service.

In Coventry the Sex Disqualification Act came to the aid of a young woman chemist, Lily Stevenson who had served an apprenticeship at her father's pharmacy. This in itself was not unprecedented but the formal presentation of her indenture papers at the Council House in 1932 meant that when her five-year training period was complete, Miss Stevenson would be eligible to become a Freeman of the City, joining the ranks of those time served men who had, for centuries, kept the privileges of the Freedom, which included a seniority pension, for themselves. There seemed to be no legal bar to the acceptance of women but there was a great deal of disquiet, the newspapers reporting that the Freemen's trustees looked upon 'this feminine invasion of their privileges with disfavour'. They were worried about 'yet another surrender to feminine infiltration' or the demolition of the 'barriers of tradition' by feminism, but their primary concern was that once women were

Miss Lily Stevenson, pharmacist, the first woman to be granted the Freedom of the city of Coventry in 1937. Here, at a reception given by the National Council of Women. *Courtesy of Coventry History Centre*

granted the Freedom, the pension pot would rapidly diminish as it was more widely shared.

When the apprenticeship was served, the City Council admitted Miss Stevenson to the Freedom of the City but the Freemen challenged the decision, seeking an injunction to stop any more women being admitted. The case attracted national attention, gaining support from organisations supporting women's professional advancement amid press stories about 'a pretty girl' who had upset and divided a city. The case rumbled on until 1944 when it was eventually dropped by the Freemen, amid fears of mounting costs.

The Second World War

When the Second World War was declared on 3 September 1939, Coventry was again poised to play a major part in the nation's war production, its factories turning out aircraft engines, a range of war materials and the machine tools required to keep industries going. As men were conscripted from the start of the war, the nation once more turned to women to do their patriotic duty and serve their country in a range of capacities. From the spring of 1941 women between 19 and 40 were compelled to register at their local employment exchanges and for the rest of that year, before the conscription of single women aged between 20 and 30 was introduced in December, there were appeals for Coventry women to take up factory work. The criticism that followed what was seen to be a slow take up, particularly among young married, childless women, must have stung. As married women, they were guaranteed local war work but in August 1941 the *Midland Daily Telegraph* accused many of wanting to go on living comfortably, 'regardless of whether our forces are receiving all the material they need or not'. The same women who had been encouraged to see their place upon marriage in the home were now harshly judged as,

> Girls who may have worked on capstans all their lives [who] suddenly discover that their cooking is perfect,

> that their husbands cannot eat any meal they have not cooked; that the excellent canteen meals provided in many places ... by trained women are unpalatable. They must be at home for this cooking.

If there was reluctance, much of it was centred on anxieties about how to shop for the family outside of working hours. In November 1941 Coventry held an exhibition on women and war work at the Central Hall, backed up with posters, a parade (one of the banner slogans urged women not to queue with the shirkers but to join the workers) and advertisements, including one using four Coventry women factory workers appealing for help and trusting women not to let them down. One of them, Winifred Shepherd, was quoted as saying, 'We women of Coventry have got a lot to say to Hitler. And the strongest way we can say it is to produce the sort of material in our local factories that hits back good and hard.'

Yet the difficulties facing women were acknowledged by the manageress of a city food shop who wrote that 'instead of organising exhibitions and parades, surely they could organise some scheme to make things easier for women to relinquish their household duties'. Evelyn Jones, who arrived in Coventry in 1939, with her husband, Jack (newly appointed as regional secretary of the Transport and General Workers' Union) and 7-week-old baby, later worked at the Standard on aircraft production. As with other mothers of children under 14, she was in fact exempt from conscription but she found enough flexibility in the job to allow her to work the morning shifts while her neighbour did the afternoons. She relied on the day nursery that opened up for pre-school children, leaving only to have her second child. Most working mothers would identify with the relief that she felt when her son complained that by being picked up at lunchtime, he was missing story time, and so he stayed on a while longer each day, allowing Evelyn to dash home, do a bit of housework and warm the house in preparation for the family's return.

Despite the persuasive advertisements, women who answered the call to take up factory work did not always feel

Second World War parade, High Street, possibly involving members of the Women's Voluntary Service, attached to the Home Guard Unit. Coventry was the first place in the country to have women Home Guards. *Courtesy of David Fry*

very welcome. Barbara Davies was a 17-year-old who came from Yorkshire to work at Armstrong Whitworth's Baginton factory and was billeted in Wyken. Her work, on the production of Lancaster bombers, was of vital importance but the arrival of the women workers did not go down well with the men who spent time playing jokes on the new recruits, sending them around the factory on fruitless missions and leaving them out of tea-making arrangements. The £5 wage Barbara had heard about back in Yorkshire was not forthcoming because, just as in the First World War, jobs were broken down into smaller parts, keeping women's rates as low as possible.

It seemed that the newspapers had forgotten that women had ever worked in factories before and needed reminding in March 1941 that 'their pretty curls can be a danger'. Without the elaborate system of welfare operating in the Coventry factories, it stated that many of the girls 'would find their coiffure a death trap'. The *Coventry Standard* explained that accidents happened when 'a girl forgets the reason for wearing [her] cap and allows it to perch at the back of her head'. Mr Yates, a local safety and welfare officer, admired the manner in which the girls were responding to the government appeal for labour; they are smart, he said, there is no question about that, 'but the very care they take with their appearance can so often mean their undoing'.

Although the priority in an industrial city was factory work, women, as in the last war, took on a wide range of roles. Barbara Davies recalled the 'glamorous' women pilots, who worked for the Auxiliary Territorial Service, coming to the factory to fly the new aircraft to airbases. There were jobs at home and away, depending on marital status, family commitments and age. Newlywed Megan Saxelby was required to give up her job in the city's department store, Owen Owen, to work in the offices at Wickman's machine tool firm, in Banner Lane, before becoming pregnant with her first child in 1944. Mrs Brown, before she was married, worked at the Co-op for much of the war until the Labour Exchange sent another girl to take her job, leaving her no choice but to move onto war work. Joining the Women's Royal Naval Service, working on the code-books from the ships and living in quarters on the south coast, she believed that the job, a chance to be independent, helped her to stand on her own two feet.

Also aged 17, Gwendoline Smith worked as a clerk for the Auxiliary Fire Service at Coventry's Central Fire Station. When the air raids began, the women clerks were also expected to work in the control room, answer calls and direct help to where it was most needed as fires broke out across the city. On the night of the Coventry Blitz, the fire station received a direct hit and the women were directed into the shelter to attend to injured firemen returning to HQ.

Although the recruitment of industrial workers remained Coventry's top priority during the war, the Council's Parks and Allotments Committee recruited from the Women's Land Army to work in the city's parks, nurseries, greenhouses and outlying farms. It was a bonus if local women were appointed because of the scarcity of lodgings in Coventry although in theory, Land Army women had to be prepared to go where they were needed. Early in the war, it was assumed that those who chose to work on the land would be women used to the outdoor or sporting life but in fact, according to the *Midland Daily Telegraph* in November 1940, 'for every riding instructress or games teacher, there are three or four housewives, shop assistants, artists and office and factory workers'. Some may have been inspired by Farm Sunday in 1943, when a procession, with a salute at the march-past taken by the mayor, Emily Smith, wove its way from the Barracks Market to the Memorial Park. As the chairwoman of the Warwickshire Land Army said in 1945, 'a hundred yards' hoeing was a hundred yards on the way to Berlin', and calls for recruits continued that year in readiness for the 'victory harvest'.

Some notable acts of bravery were publicly acknowledged; Mary Beardsall, a nursing orderly at Coventry and Warwickshire Hospital, nurse Margaret Brown and matron Joyce Burton, were among those who received the George Cross for saving patients' lives during the April 1941 air raid in which the hospital was hit by a high explosive bomb. Mary Beardsall was on duty all night and fought and subdued a fire on the top floor of the hospital single handed. Despite being injured by falling debris, she then entered a damaged ward to rescue several people trapped by the debris, then continued with her duties, before being injured again, this time severely, returning to her job after ten weeks in hospital.

As in the First World War, women came from Ireland to work. A city councillor raised concerns about Irish nurses working in the city's hospitals and unable to travel home for their holidays after the government had imposed a travel ban between Britain and Ireland in 1943. The Chairman of the Public Health Service replied that he would do whatever he could to help the situation, stressing how important it was that young women from Ireland were not put off coming to work in Coventry.

For many women, in war as in peacetime, it was the juggling of roles that was the most difficult to manage, combining caring for children or relations with part time paid or unpaid war work. The work of the Women's Voluntary Service (WVS) under the local leadership of city councillor Pearl Hyde, included help and support for those bombed out of their homes, the provision of meals and clothes, sewing, knitting and visits to air raid shelters and assistance in hospitals and reception centres. The WVS had a clothing depot and received requests for those who had lost everything during raids, including equipment for a new born baby, bedding for a German refugee and underwear for a child who was being evacuated. Food was prepared in what became known as the 'Devil's Kitchen' in the basement of the Police Station. When a bomb fell on the station in 1941, the B Division of the WVS carried on with their duties and when someone came to check on them, he was astonished to find them wearing an assortment of saucepans and colanders on their heads because they had never been issued with helmets. Mobile canteens were sent all over the city, to emergency feeding centres, rest centres and factories. Days after the April 1941 raid, here is a typical canteen report:

> Eight am reported for duty, stocked up nine-ten am. Nine fifty five am sent to Park Road and Radford District, on to Alvis Works, GEC Works, Carmelite Road and Gulson Road, back to GEC Works. Returned one ten pm, GEC no good. One forty pm sent to Warwick Row, Food Control and then to Sibree Hall. Business good. Five thirty pm returned.

A later report reveals that the Canteens were supplied with two boilers full of hot stew and 210 dozen cheese, salmon and meat sandwiches, with the instruction from the Ministry of Food to give out the food free of charge until evening.

One evening a young Coventry woman on her way home from playing tennis with friends, came across a dance for soldiers and was invited in by Pearl Hyde. They all went in wearing their sports gear and had a lovely evening, the young woman declaring that if this was the WVS, she was very happy

Lady Reading, National President of the Women's Voluntary Service, seated centre front row with members of the Coventry WVS and (next to her, hatless) Mrs Pearl Hyde, local WVS organiser. *Courtesy of the Herbert Art Gallery & Museum, Coventry*

to join. She was a bit shocked to find that her first job was not quite such fun and involved knocking on doors in Coventry to find out who would take munitions workers in as boarders. Lists were made of beds available and there was a column for notes such as, 'Very Good Home. Musical', 'Very Fair. Wines and Spirits' or 'Clean, well-furnished, good amenities, keen on antiques'. Nonetheless, she enjoyed being part of a small group often referred to as Pearl Hyde's glamour girls and, combining WVS duties with paid work, had 'a lovely war'. Other women in the WVS wondered what on earth they would do with their spare time when the war ended.

Post-war Work

The end of the war was greeted with the same mixture of relief and anxieties for the future as in 1918. There was disruption, dislocation and unemployment when war production ended; Barbara Davies, along with the other women war workers at Armstrong Whitworth, was sacked immediately after VJ Day in August 1945 and there was, she remembered, a real sense of rejection among the women who were simply expected to go back to wherever they had come from. There were mixed messages for women in the post-war years. On one hand, there was a strong expectation that they would embrace the roles of wives and mothers or resume traditional pre-war types of women's work. On the other, there was an urgent need for women's involvement in the country's manufacturing industries and many of Coventry's trades, notably the car industry, played a key part in the nation's recovery. The compromise for many women was to take on part-time work across a whole range of sectors, including manufacturing and service industries, the newly created National Health Service and in the professions. Nevertheless, marriage bars, largely temporarily suspended during the war, were back in the 1950s and the Equal Pay Act (implemented in January 1976) was still a long way off. Most women's lives continued to be influenced by society's expectations of them as carers and home makers, supported by men and ready to give up paid work when children came along. But, throughout our hundred-year period, there were many women who did not conform to these norms.

I want to conclude with the story of Evelyn Evans, born in Coventry in 1910. She attended Barr's Hill Secondary School and on leaving, joined the city's library service. She took her professional exams by correspondence course, learning while working, until she became a branch library assistant and then Inspector of Branch Libraries, before moving to York as its Deputy City Librarian. In 1935 she had her first experience of working abroad, organising an exchange year with the University of Michigan, one of the first librarians to do so and taking every opportunity while there to travel. In 1945 the *Coventry Evening Telegraph* reported that Evelyn sailed for the Gold Coast (Ghana since 1957) to take up the position of British Council librarian. When she left in 1965, it was as the country's highly regarded Director of Library Services. Some years earlier, as the service expanded, she needed to recruit two deputies and was advised to hire women because a man 'will be after your job'.

'No, he won't', replied Evelyn, 'because it's my job'.

CHAPTER THREE

At Home

In January 1917, a plea from the Reverend Bainton of the West Orchard Congregational Church summed up the hopes being pinned on women when the war ended, emphasising their unchanging primary moral and domestic responsibilities. When the boys come home from the Front, their hearts beating with thankfulness as they cross the threshold, how will they be greeted?

> Will everything be in order for their homecoming? Will the wife be at her best, clean, well dressed, attractive and as pretty in her make up as she used to be in the days of love's sweet dream? Or will the place be found, like so many have the misfortune to discover it when they return from their daily work weary, hungry for comfort and repose, all in confusion with washing and ironing in full swing, nauseous from the heat of the steam and the smell of the soap; the children grimy and ill-clad, the wife in ragged skirt and hair in curlers; the whole atmosphere of home uncongenial and unpleasant?

This, suggested the Reverend, was women's 'great and grave responsibility' because a 'well-ordered domestic life is the foundation of all social well-being'. Women have,

> sagacity and virtues such as few men have. They have a clearer and more correct comprehension of family

> responsibilities. Their moral sense is keen, their taste is better, their views are higher. That is why home comfort and home attractiveness depend upon them more than upon the men. If they fail, then our case is a poor one indeed.

Although Bainton spoke at a time of national crisis, the message was a familiar one. If men belonged in the world of industry and now of war, then women's world – whatever else they did – was still centred on the home. Throughout the hundred years covered in this book, the voices were constant, insistent and hard to ignore – women should marry, they should have children, they should be dedicated wives, sensible mothers and excellent housewives. If men claimed the outside world as theirs, then surely the indoor world was the woman's domain, with freedom to look after herself and her family as she saw best.

But the voices seldom stopped at telling women what to do; they often told her how to do it – when to marry (not too young, but don't leave it too late), how to keep her husband happy (pipe and slippers at the ready), how to be the

Daddy at the War. Postcard sent from France during the First World War. *Author's own collection*

perfect mother (more than likely to remind her that she wasn't doing it right), how to cook, clean and shop. In January 1939 the *Midland Daily Telegraph* ran an article which sought to encourage women to regard shopping not as a task but as an adventure; it advised that, with time and attention devoted to it, it was possible to become a good shopper rather than one who potters and then makes a bad bargain or who shops recklessly in the sales. Learn your job, women were told; if you don't know which cuts of meat to choose, read up on it before you shop, or ask the butcher. Examine everything before you buy; not only is this sensible, it will earn the respect of the tradesmen.

The expectation was that women would conform to the domestic ideal. This chapter looks behind those expectations, from the domestic happiness that many women sought, to the tensions caused by the 'double shift' of paid work and running the home. Some found happiness and fulfilment in the role of homemaker, for others the reality was very different.

The banner headlines in the national press when the 1921 Census was published tell us a great deal about how society viewed the importance of marriage for women. It revealed that there were almost two million more women than men in the country and clearly – tragically and shockingly – that meant that some of these 'surplus' women in the post-war years would end up without husbands. Single women were made to feel ridiculous by the press, portrayed as desperate man-chasers and given advice on how to find husbands, even if it meant emigrating in order to do so. It had to be done; it was there in black and white – there could be no happiness for women without marriage, only frustration and dealing with other people's pity for the rest of their lives.

Weddings

Descriptions and photos of weddings show us that fashions may have changed over the years but it is fair to assume that wedding days remained one of the most memorable and glamorous of family occasions. There was always considerable

The wedding of Coventry couple Fred and Mabel Hancox in 1901. *Courtesy of Albert Smith*

public interest in what the bride and bridesmaids wore, with detailed descriptions carried in the local press throughout the period. When Gertrude Langley (who we met in Chapter Two as Mrs Walter Beamish, VAD Quarter Master for Warwick 70 Division) married in September 1914, the *Midland Daily Telegraph* informed readers that she did so in a dress of ivory satin Charmeuse, with a ninon bodice and a skirt draped with Carrick Macrosse lace. Loaned by her mother-in-law (along with the lace), the dress was embroidered with pearls and the Court train of white ninon was lined with pale pink ninon, one corner being turned up with orange blossom and a true lovers' knot of pearls. Her veil was of white tulle, with sprays of orange blossom in her hair and she carried a sheaf of lilies and pale pink carnations. Presents given to the happy couple, who honeymooned in Devon, were said to be numerous and valuable. Fashions were carefully followed but in January 1915, a trend for bareheaded bridesmaids seems to have upset a Bedworth vicar who, despite the mounting tensions of war,

The 1918 wedding at Exhall Parish Church of Sgt E Martin, MM, and Nurse WF Carpenter. The bride arrived at the church with Surgeon-Major Orton and left with her husband. *Coventry Graphic*, 22 February 1918. *Courtesy of Coventry History Centre*

was anxious enough to write to the press to complain this was neither seemly or becoming and pointing out that it was as disrespectful to the congregation and as irreverent as regards God as it would be if a woman came to church on Sunday without a hat.

When the events of war threatened a bride's special day, it was simply a case of getting on with it. Arranged during her fiance's home-leave, Megan Saxelby's wedding took place on 9 April 1941, the night after a devastating air raid on Coventry. Megan spent the night in the family's Anderson shelter and emerged in the morning with time just to grab her wedding clothes and leave her parents' house, a delayed-action bomb having fallen close by. She was given a lift to nearby Meriden, where her future parents in law had lived since being bombed out of their Radford house in November 1940. Here, she had some sleep while her family checked on the vicar and made sure that St Nicholas Church Hall in Coventry (licenced for weddings since the destruction of the church the previous year) was still intact. There could be no bridal cars as the company they had chosen could not get its cars out because there was an unexploded bomb right outside. But the ceremony went ahead, complete with flowers somehow delivered on time and a worn out vicar who had been working through the night offering comfort to those affected by the raid.

Megan Saxelby, whose wedding took place on 9 April, 1941. Here, she is standing in front of the family air raid shelter, neatly disguised as a rockery. *Courtesy of Megan Saxelby*

When planned weddings did not take place, the sense of betrayal and humiliation were keenly felt. It is hard to underestimate the courage of Amy Hurlston who sued her ex-fiancé, Mr Theodore Edmond, for breach of contract when he broke off their engagement just a month before the wedding in 1897. The ceremony was due to take place at the Catholic Brompton Oratory in London and the bride to be had converted to her fiance's faith in preparation. Although Miss Hurlston sought £5,000 in damages, the case was settled before it was heard in court and the jury accepted the instruction from the solicitor to accept £1,050 plus costs from Mr Edmond. Had the full case been heard in court, the press would have disclosed all sorts of details of the couple's private lives and I rather suspect there was a local sense of disappointment that the public was denied these. Perhaps

Miss Hurlston was encouraged in her actions by her membership of the Women's Emancipation Union, formed in the 1890s to secure 'the Political, Social and Economic Independence of Women' as well as equality in marriage and parenthood. As we saw in Chapter Two, she was already an independent woman at the time of the proposed marriage, making a living out of writing. In 1892, when her father's watchmaking business ran into trouble, a meeting of creditors found that Amy had lent her father a considerable sum of money and was now willing to forgo her claim so that other creditors could be paid. A situation in which an unmarried daughter came to the financial aid of a proud, independent artisan providing for his family certainly does not fit the image presented by Charles Bray in the 1850s and may well have been a bitter pill for Mr Hurlston to swallow.

For Better or Worse…

Between 1850 and 1950, women's expectations of marriage changed, along with laws giving them greater rights over their own children, allowing them to keep their own inheritances and earnings and divorce their husbands on the same terms as they were able to be divorced by men. Nonetheless, they continued to be brought up to believe that their working lives would be short and that marriage was the goal. To be left on the shelf was pitiable and to live with a man outside of a formal union was nothing short of scandalous. When George Eliot, by then living in London, began a cohabitation with George Lewes in 1854, her Coventry friend, Cara, wife of Charles Bray, could not bring herself to speak or write to her for several years. This was despite the fact that the radical Brays themselves had a somewhat unconventional marriage, during which Charles openly had affairs, with him and his wife adopting one of the children born as a consequence.

In Victorian Britain, it was assumed that marriage made wives financially dependent on their husbands. Even if he desired it, the prospect of a Coventry weaver being the sole provider for his wife and family was largely elusive. As we have seen, it was generally regarded as advantageous for a male weaver in Coventry to marry in order to be able to work with his wife to build up the workshop business. They might, if possible, try to avoid having children until they had savings enough to buy or rent their own loom but then, as the family grew, every child played a vital part in sustaining the family weaving business. There was criticism for those who it was considered had married too young. When Joseph Gutteridge married his first wife, Sarah, in 1835, he was 20 and she was just 16. He had not yet completed his weaving apprenticeship and was severely admonished by his relations and his employers who saw his marriage as a premature and foolhardy step. As a result, no help was forthcoming for the young couple when they fell more than once on hard times; his firm would not keep him on once his apprenticeship was complete and all the while their family was expanding before there was any possibility of having their own loom. Their poverty was exacerbated by poor housing, prolonged illnesses and the death of their fourth child from smallpox and from Gutteridge's reluctance to take jobs

An example of the inadequacy of much of Coventry's central housing. These are old timbered houses, condemned and voluntarily closed in 1899 before improvements were made in 1900. Annual Report Coventry Medical Officer of Health, 1900. *Courtesy of Coventry History Centre*

he believed were beneath him and his absolute refusal to apply for parish relief because, 'I would have rather have died from sheer starvation than, being so young, have degraded myself'. All this took its toll on his wife who died, aged just 36, from tuberculosis and Gutteridge realising that Sarah, of 'high moral worth and patient loving nature' had 'overtaxed her strength in ministering so patiently and faithfully to the needs of her partner in life'.

From the nineteenth right through to the twentieth century, the reality of a working-class husband being able to earn enough money for his entire family rested to a large extent on good fortune. When lean times or disaster struck, families needed to pull together, taking work wherever it was available. Mrs Dingley's father worked in the cycle trade before the First World War and when he was laid off in the slack season, her mother would scrub floors or black-lead grates to help make ends meet. When husbands were ill or on short time, children of earning age knew how vital their contribution to housekeeping was and handed money over every week so that the rent could be paid. One woman born in a poor part of the city recalled how important it was to her to show the landlord when he came round to collect the rent that despite the poverty they were alright, and so she would place flowers on the table and tidy up in readiness. Maintaining standards was a question of pride but was extremely difficult in the face of landlords such as hers, who took the rent but had no interest in the property, refusing to decorate or undertake running repairs.

The death of a husband could spell financial disaster for a working class woman with dependent children. Before 1925, there was no state pension scheme for widows and so, in order to keep the family together, many widowed mothers had no choice but to take whatever work they could. One woman, born in East Street in 1892, lost her father when she was 5;

> Of course my mother had to bring five of us up and she had to go scrubbing and washing and everything else, but anyway we was alright, we just didn't owe anybody

> anything or anything like that. And if she hadn't got the money we didn't have it. She wouldn't ever go into debt my mum wouldn't do.

This was the alternative to the workhouse for, when the mother asked the Poor Law Guardians for help, they refused any relief except admittance to the workhouse, to which she replied, 'thank you sir, good morning'. Her resourcefulness was long remembered by her family; she would boil a pig's head and make soup out of it. She was, said her daughter, 'a darling. Angel on earth ... what she said was law but she still loved every one of us'. May Purnell remembered her mother serving dinners of rabbit, pig's tail, 'a lovely big stew' or suet pudding, always making sure that her children were well fed.

When family allowances were at last introduced by the Labour government in 1946, many mothers saw them as a lifeline, even though the amounts paid (for all but the first child, clearly in the hope that couples would see it as an incentive to have more children, thereby raising the birth rate) were nowhere near those hoped for by those who had long campaigned for mothers' economic independence. Yet the payments were at least assured, regular, and made a very significant contribution to the family budget.

The Workhouse

Although the workhouse was no one's idea of home, it provided shelter to many families from the beginning of our period until 1929 when the Poor Law was finally abolished and its infirmary passed into the hands of the City Council as a municipal hospital. When no one else could help, when all other avenues had been explored, the workhouse reared its head, its inmates enduring a tough regime of separating parents from children, of working (if you were fit) and with few opportunities to break the monotony and forget the shame that accompanied being an official pauper. Conditions in the workhouse were intentionally harsh in order to remind people of the importance of solvency

Coventry Workhouse, at the city end of London Road. Opened in 1801, the photograph was taken in the 1920s. This section of the workhouse was originally a Carmelite (Whitefriars) friary. *Courtesy of Coventry History Centre*

within a society that often did not understand the causes of poverty and chose to distinguish between those considered deserving and those who were merely feckless or degenerate. Deserted wives and children were more likely to be taken into the workhouse than given 'out relief' - to help them remain in the home (if indeed this was even an option) - because of the suspicion that the desertion might not be genuine and was instead a ruse to get hold of some extra cash.

In *Hurdy Gurdy Days*, the story of Mrs Graves is told. She endured years of violent abuse at the hands of her drunkard husband, bearing many children, most of whom did not live long. The whole neighbourhood was scared of Mr Graves and, as was common in cases of domestic violence, no one intervened when he beat his wife or threw her out of the house and eventually, exhausted and ill with nowhere else to go, she went into the workhouse. After she died, Mr Graves' health deteriorated as

Coventry Workhouse. The room shown here was also used as a dormitory by the friars 400 years earlier. *Courtesy of Coventry History Centre*

he drank more and more heavily and could no longer work. He found that no one offered him any help even when his cries of pain were heard across the court and he died in the workhouse infirmary. A community response of sorts, I suppose.

The Admissions' Registers for Coventry Workhouse show what a struggle it was for families to recover from destitution. In the late 1890s 35-year-old Elizabeth was admitted into Coventry Workhouse with six of her children, aged between 10 years and 6 months. Over the next two years, there were numerous discharges and readmissions for Elizabeth who sometimes had to leave one or more of her children behind in the workhouse until her circumstances improved. On one occasion, one of her sons was removed from the workhouse by his grandmother but was back in again for a spell the following year. Elizabeth's story, like so many others, is hard to piece together; described in the Admissions' book as a schoolteacher and wife, she did not enter the workhouse with her husband. Although her youngest child was baptised in Coventry, her other children were born in London and there is no information about why the move took place. The three eldest, aged between 17 and 13 – probably already earning – did not come into the workhouse with their mother. By 1901, Elizabeth was living in Hillfields with her mother, who was a domestic worker. These two, described as widows, provided a home for those of Elizabeth's children who were still dependent on them. In 1911 they lived in a congested part of the city centre, both women employed in industry. It was a tough existence.

In the early twentieth century, one Coventry daughter fully understood her mother's meaning when she told her not to bring trouble home, or it would be the workhouse for her, a legacy of nineteenth-century attitudes that unmarried mothers should be admitted to the workhouse rather than helped in the community, thereby emphasising their shame. Once in the workhouse, the jobs assigned to an unmarried mother were more unpleasant than those of other women and nor was she supposed to attend church outside the workhouse on Sundays. With the arrival of the first women Poor Law Guardians from the 1890s, it is sometimes possible to see a softening of attitudes; in 1907 Mrs Sarah Griffiths was elected as a Labour Guardian in Coventry. The following year, she commented on the highly publicised case of a young unmarried laundry worker who had allegedly asphyxiated her infant child after giving birth alone in lodgings in London. At her trial the woman, Daisy Lord, was found guilty of murder and given the death penalty, later commuted to life imprisonment, and campaigners then sought a further reduction in the term. The case generated a great deal of sympathy for those 'betrayed and deserted' by men who escaped justice. Sarah Griffiths wrote to the *Woman Worker*, a trade union paper for women,

> As a member of the Board of Guardians, I know something of the suffering of these poor girls, and how hard it is for them to lift their heads again after they have once fallen. To see them try to get someone to take care of their little mites, so that they may be able to support themselves and the baby, has often made my heart ache. Some are successful and get out; but what about the poor girls who have no friends? They are compelled to spend months shut up in the workhouse, and their one cry is "Cannot you get me out of this place? I shall go mad if I stay much longer!"

Bricks and Mortar

As Coventry's population grew, so did the need for good quality accommodation for its workers and their families. When manufacturers and professional people prospered, they increasingly left the houses of the cramped city centre and instead built larger ones out of town, in Stoke, in the new suburb of Earlsdon (brought into the city boundary in 1890) or beyond. Apart from a few pockets of relative splendour, such as the Quadrant and Warwick Row, from 1850 onwards the city centre became a congested hotchpotch of residential and industrial premises, interspersed with shops, warehouses and slaughterhouses. The gardens of the large houses built in earlier centuries were built upon, squeezing in small cottages with no direct access onto the road and instead facing onto courtyards where there was

A cottage in a Coventry court, closed 1902. Annual Report Coventry Medical Officer of Health, 1902. *Courtesy of Coventry History Centre*

a single standpipe and with cesspits just feet from the front doors. The smallest of these cottages had just one room up, one down, providing housing for people in the central districts surrounding St Johns Street, Gosford Street and Spon Street. There was a great deal of overcrowding in these cramped and poorly ventilated 'courts', where epidemics including scarlet fever, typhus and diarrhoea pushed mortality rates above the national average (see Chapter Four for more on this).

By the end of the nineteenth century, the courts were among Coventry's worst housing and were slow to be cleared away, with many surviving well into the twentieth century. Legislation existed to condemn and close houses regarded as unfit for habitation but it was not until 1930 that the Council was in a position to develop a five year plan not just to clear but to replace slum dwellings. As preparations were made to clear the houses in the Chauntry Place area, between Cook Street and Hales Street, tenants were offered newly built municipal housing in Stoke Aldermoor. Many of Chauntry Place's 147 houses were between 100 and 150 years old, grouped together around courtyards.

St Agnes Lane, between Cook Street and Hales Street and parallel with Chauntry Place. In this picture taken in the 1930s, demolition is under way. *Courtesy of Coventry History Centre*

The Council report found that the majority had perished brick work, porous walls and bulging walls, defective roofs and no damp-proof courses. Houses were often without ventilated larders and so foodstuffs had to be stored in dark, damp cupboards or boxes; 116 of the houses were without sinks and only eight had lavatories. Only eleven of the houses had their own water supply and most tenants relied on water from outside standpipes or yard taps in the courts, with wastewater emptied into gullies into the streets. Outside lavatories were shared, between maybe four to fourteen houses. Women had to take it in turns to use the washing lines in the courts so there was invariably wet washing competing for space with playing children, dustbins and neighbours making trips to the lavatories. Bringing up children here was undeniably hard; May Purnell, born in 1903, remembered carrying in water from the communal tap on washdays and bath days, particularly punishing in winter when the supply would freeze. Wastewater flowed into a drain just outside the house, cleaned out on a Saturday morning but costing May's mother a small fortune in Jeyes Fluid to keep the smell and the germs away from her family. Sisters and mother slept together in one room; there was just a paraffin lamp downstairs by which to do mending and the rain would seep in through the roof after a gale.

By the early twentieth century, Chauntry Place had acquired a bad reputation, largely because of the state of its housing and negligent landlords but what May saw was a community where everyone knew and looked out for each other; 'we liked it', she said, 'we grew up with it'; she remembered the Chauntry boys lost in the First World War, to whom a memorial was taken to Holy Trinity Church.

There was sadness at leaving behind caring communities, but for many women the promise of more space, a front room *and* a kitchen, an inside water supply and perhaps a bathroom, was enough to persuade them to move their families to the Council estates that eventually replaced the slums or to private rented housing if it was affordable. In *Hurdy Gurdy Days*, Grace Charlton's mother overcame her husband and mother-in-law's objections to leaving their home in Much Park Street where they had lived all their lives. Finding the courage to speak to the man who was building new houses on what became the Charterhouse estate, she found out that the houses were to be sold for £180, but that some would be subsequently let by landlords for 5*s* 9*d* a week, over 2*s* more than they were already struggling to pay. Not only that, but the landlord would demand a week's rent in advance. Despite the odds, Mrs Charlton made the move a reality, marking 'the beginning of our changed world'.

By the end of the First World War, it was clear that Coventry was in dire need of decent and affordable housing. The Stoke Heath housing estate, built for munitions workers during the war with the aid of a government grant, was owned by the council, but questions and discussions about the planning and building of more municipal housing remained urgent. Labour Councillor Ellen Hughes (one of the two first women councillors elected in Coventry in 1919) was keen to stress the needs of families; along with the importance of providing space and amenities, she wanted all houses to have baths. To deal with 'the incessant chasing away of dirt', she wanted women to have hot water heating in the new houses but in order for this to happen, it would be necessary to

Some of Coventry's first Council houses, in Narrow Lane, Foleshill, built in 1908. Annual Report Coventry Medical Officer of Health, 1910. *Courtesy of Coventry History Centre*

improve Coventry's water, which was so hard that it corroded the pipes in a very short time. Kitchens needed dressers and built-in cupboards, despite the fact that her male colleagues thought that the latter were an unnecessary expense. There must be space for children to play safely, away from the roads and Councillor Hughes wanted to see estates provided with centres where children over the age of 2 could play, looked after by trained nurses.

Councillor Hughes was rightly impatient for change; by 1927 there were over 5,000 people on the Council housing waiting list and too few municipal homes being built. The development of the Radford Garden Suburb, with 2,500 houses completed by 1939, eased some pressure. There was, however, an enormous amount of private building going on in

Stoke Heath housing estate was built with Government assistance, originally for workers during the First World War. *Courtesy of David Fry*

the city before the Second World War and although builders imagined that the properties would be bought up by landlords as investments, a vast number of properties were bought by Coventry families, many stretching their budgets to the limit in order to have somewhere to live. One Coventry woman was only about 16 when she first saw the house of her dreams, with 'lovely little red tiles in the hall, shiny ones, not brick, and there was the hall … and the bathroom … three lovely bedrooms, oh, I thought it was heaven'. Later, when married, the couple saved the £100 needed to put down on the house; '…a ten shilling note went in a tin, a pound note went in a tin, you've no idea, nobody on earth would ever know, how hard it was to save a hundred pounds', only to realise that wasn't enough with solicitors' fees and moving costs. When they did move in, they were worse off than when they had paid rent on rooms and new furniture and fittings for the house had to wait. But it was theirs.

Communal Living

Home was not always the conventional family unit. During wartime, some single women experienced life away from home for the first time, in lodgings or hostels. In 1916 a report into welfare conditions among women workers in Coventry stressed the importance of getting this experiment in communal living right, especially when 'long narrow rows of barrack-like buildings are not attractive to British girls in whom, fortunately, the instinct of home is strong'. It drew attention to objections such as canteens offering no meal choices, no quiet sitting room areas and no easy chairs in the sleeping cubicles, for women to read or write letters home. As more hostels were built, lessons were learned; passages became wider, comforts provided and surroundings made brighter. One Ordnance worker recalled that the canteen was always spotless, there were maids to tidy and keep jugs in the bedrooms filled with water for washing and the hostel accommodated the different shifts worked.

First World War Coventry munition workers' hostel. *Courtesy of David Fry*

> So when we got up in the afternoon your tea was always ready for you. So you could get up and have a bath if you wanted to. Now, they had a big recreation room which was beautiful and there were places for you to write letters with all your facilities in that room. And then the other room was a big huge dance room and there was a piano there and they used to run dances at night times.

The importance of providing safe and affordable lodgings for women workers had arisen before the First World War. Campaigners were concerned that for women unable to remain in the family home, low wages meant that they lost out to men who got better lodgings and in the nicest locations. Poor Law Guardian Sarah Griffiths wanted three municipal hostels close

Girls' Friendly Society Lodge, 'Brooklyn', Foleshill Road, opened in 1915.
Courtesy of David Fry

to women's employment and each to be provided with a foster mother who would take a practical interest in the girls' moral and physical wellbeing. These did not materialise but the Girls' Friendly Society (established nationally by Anglicans in 1875) collected in the city for years until it had the funds to buy a large house, Brooklyn, on Foleshill Road, promising good lodgings and recreation rooms where women could safely spend their free time. The Lodge opened in 1915 for thirty-six boarders in twelve bedrooms. During the war most of its residents were munitions workers (a Welfare Inspector finding the premises to be 'most efficient, charmingly equipped and arranged'), one of whom, Miss Swatridge, was awarded the OBE for acting with 'great braveness and promptness' when some fuses at the Ordnance exploded. She was one of five sisters from Devon who lived at the Lodge over a period of three years. After the war several residents were women who came to teach in the city's schools and there was also accommodation and domestic service training for young girls sent to the Lodge by the Board of Guardians. The religious and moral tone of the Girls' Friendly Society, which required church attendance on Sundays, was, however, not popular with all and by 1923 the dwindling number of boarders was causing anxiety.

St Faith's Shelter

Margaret Paton arrived in Coventry before the Second World War to work at St Faith's Shelter, at that time housed in an old watchmaker's workshop on Holyhead Road. Affiliated to the Diocesan Society for Purity, its mission was to give a temporary home to vulnerable and friendless young women, some of whom were expectant or single mothers. In 1934 the Society wrote that,

> There is one mistake which people make about our Shelter, and that is that it is only for 'naughty girls'. This is by no means right. We are here to help anyone in need, whether it is work, shelter or advice that they

> are requiring, and just because a girls applies for work from our address it does not necessarily follow that she has been in trouble or difficulties of any kind. Even for those who have acted stupidly in the past and made their mistakes, it is far more often than not due to bad influence and wrong surroundings than to real wickedness.

Domestic training was strongly encouraged to enable women 'to become useful members of society' and babies were sent to foster parents so that mothers could go into service, while still providing for their children. The Superintendent ensured that the women who came to the Shelter were always treated with thoughtfulness and kindness. Both their privacy and their freedom were respected and, despite limited resources, the importance of decent, wholesome food was recognised, ignoring old fashioned, judgemental notions that restricting meat in the diets of 'wayward' girls would avoid 'feeding the animal' in them. On the night of the Coventry Blitz, young women and babies went into the cellar. With no water or gas supplies, they were left to heat babies' bottles over a candle fetched from the chapel. This was followed by evacuation to South Warwickshire and after the war, a new home at Dudley Lodge on Warwick Road and,

> How thankful we are to be comfortably settled in a warm house, fitted central heating and a cosy nursery – which is never empty – how some of the little mites weighing just over five pounds would have fared without it in the bitter weather is not hard to imagine.

A senior midwife, Mrs Delia Fell, recalled the continued compassion and support offered by St Faith's wardens to women who had no support from their families, offering help to find work that allowed single mothers to support their babies when state help was so inadequate.

Little Park Street after the Coventry Blitz on the night of 14 November 1940. *Courtesy of Coventry History Centre*

War Damage

After the Coventry Blitz on 14 November 1940, 5,500 families were evacuated from the city. Nearly 43,000 houses were damaged or destroyed, amounting to fifty-six per cent of the city's housing stock. In the house where Evelyn Jones lived with her family, a bomb fell in the back garden; the kitchen was destroyed and the ceilings brought down by blast. It was, said Evelyn, in words no doubt echoed by thousands, 'chaos', but 'I don't think I've ever had much feeling for possessions since then, because at least the next morning we were still a family'.

The post-war challenges were enormous and temporary measures included the construction of over a thousand prefabricated houses. Even so, people lived in hostels, on disused army sites, as well as in caravans and railway carriages on bombsites. Solicitor Bill Wilson, who later became a Coventry Labour MP, recalled the occasion when he represented a young

A family living at Meriden Camp, 1942. They may have been displaced by the raids or among those who chose to get out of the city at night time. *Courtesy of the Herbert Art Gallery & Museum, Coventry*

woman who had given birth in a caravan because she had not been allowed to go into the maternity hospital. What impressed him was the interest taken by a woman alderman, Alice Arnold, who, not content with merely discussing the case in a committee meeting, had gone to see what conditions for the mother were like – the only member of the committee to have done so. Reminiscent of Councillor Ellen Hughes' emphasis on practical detail, this was typical of Alice Arnold's insistence on improved living conditions for Coventry families. When the plans for the city's reconstructed centre were underway, she protested at the precedence she felt that the Council was giving to shops before sufficient action had been taken to improve housing, education and social services.

What's for Tea?

Trying to capture a hundred years of women looking after the family and the home has made me realise how little the routine and the necessity of planning and providing has changed over the generations. My children have grown up and gone their own ways but still, at a certain point in my working day, my thoughts drift to 'what are we going to eat tonight'? One day, I remember bumping into my friend Rachel, who, like me, was dropping off her eldest at school and as we turned for home, with toddlers in pushchairs, she turned to me and said the words that summed up our thoughts then and pretty well forever – 'another day, another tea'.

Whether they liked it or not, there is little doubt that most married women were responsible for shopping, cooking and keeping the house in order and those seen to fall down on these duties, however restricted they were by budget, were harshly judged. In the very first issue of the GEC's *Loudspeaker* magazine, in 1924, women were reminded – in language that could easily have belonged in 1850 – that in order for the home to be a place of happiness, 'exercising beneficial influences upon its members – and especially upon the children growing up within it – the home must be pervaded by the spirit of comfort, cleanliness, affection and intelligence'. At the heart of this, 'the presence of a well-ordered, industrious, and educated woman is indispensable. So much depends upon the woman, that we might almost pronounce the happiness or unhappiness of the home to be woman's work'. There was no escaping the advice to housewives in the women's magazines which proliferated in the inter-war years, but to find it also in the works' magazine – particularly in one that made a point of printing regular profiles of its women workers – must surely have got under the skin of some women.

All that domestic economy training at school was clearly expected to ensure that a woman could whip up a good hearty meal with whatever ingredients were available to her and whatever her budget. Then, as now, critics were inclined to forget the additional costs of fuel and cooking equipment; in the poorest of households, it was not uncommon to have just one pot or pan for all cooking (sometimes doubling up for other tasks, such as soaking and boil washing clothes) and insufficient crockery and cutlery for the whole family, meaning that it was not just cheaper to rely on bread-based meals but easier to serve and eat them too.

Shopping for many items was a daily task, cutting into time already needed for household work, not to mention cooking. In order to get the best cuts of meat, it was important to arrive at the butcher's shop or market stall as soon as possible after opening in the morning, but many oral testimonies are of getting hold of cheap meat at the end of the week. A Coventry woman, born in 1912, remembered that her granny used to come and sit with the children so that her mum and dad could go to the market around nine o'clock on Saturday night when they were practically giving meat away, so that the family always had a good joint for Sunday, with the remainder 'stewed up, hashed up, and all that sort of thing' for the rest of the week. Mrs Emes, born in 1908, recalled Friday night auctions when it was possible to get discounted fruit, vegetables and sometimes fish and bacon that would then last the week. Some butchers would allow customers to buy joints and leave them in the shop meat safe until Sunday morning.

Despite the arrival of gas ovens, which households were able to rent from the early 1900s, the supply of gas was not always terribly efficient. Dorothy McLatchie was interviewed by the Hillfields History Group and recalled collapsed cakes and the need to get up very early on Christmas Day because the entire neighbourhood would be cooking;

> You'd have to put it in the oven hours before you needed it, because the pressure would be so low. You'd probably have to get up at about 7 o'clock to get the chicken in for 8 o'clock and you'd be very lucky if it was cooked for 2 o'clock.

Shopping and cooking for a family was challenging even when work and food were plentiful. To do so in times of acute hardship or crisis was extremely stressful. Coventry women were no strangers to soup kitchens which were established during times of hardship, for example, when the ribbon trade suffered a severe slump in 1860 and then in the early 1920s when unemployment was high. At these times, food supplies funded by the public and by the Council ensured at least some nourishment to the worst affected families.

Wartime in particular sorely tried the patience of women looking after families. The cost of living rose steeply during the First World War; it was estimated that the average working-class household saw its expenditure on food increase by ninety per cent in four years and other costs, including fuel and lighting, went up by as much as seventy-four per cent. Many women found that they could not manage on the army separation allowance and had to look for work to supplement the family income. Although decent amounts of money could be earned in the munitions factories, those who worked in more traditional jobs, such as laundry and catering, remained on much lower wages.

Coventry Communal kitchen, formally opened on 19 October, 1917 in St Mary's Hall to help conserve the city's food supplies. Rationing was introduced from January 1918. *Courtesy of David Fry*

Rationing arrived in Britain early in 1918 but before then, Coventry had seen a great deal of anger at the alleged profits that some shopkeepers were making and at suspicions that those with the most money were getting their hands on more than a fair share of available foodstuffs and hoarding them. It was reported that housewives had to travel to nearby towns in order to buy food. At a Pool Meadow demonstration of up to 50,000 people in November 1917, one speaker announced that 'the time has arrived when people in this city have pockets full of money and are not able to buy food'. While many women might have wondered about the pockets of money, exasperation was certainly felt – as in the Second World War – at the near impossibility of getting hold of foods in short supply by the time the working day was over. In 1918, in protest at this, Mrs Bonham and Mrs Carter who worked together on the trams, interrupted the morning's service, forcing the inspector to get in touch with the mayor, who issued the women crews with tickets entitling them to go to the front of the queue in shops during their 'rest' periods.

In May 1917 a communal kitchen opened in St Mary's Hall and the following year a municipal restaurant was established in the former skating rink in Ford Street, transformed into an attractive dining hall, surrounded by a well-equipped kitchen. Customers could choose whether to eat in or to take dishes home with them, so that they could save on gas and coal and the city could do its best to make food economies, because 'Economy Means Victory: Save Food, Save Fuel, Save Labour'. The hope was that such ventures would reduce the anxieties of shopping and cooking and the *Midland Daily Telegraph* hoped that even 'if the national temper does not improve through them, the national physique should'. One Monday's fare in November was haricot bean soup for a penny, a beef cutlet for two pence, potatoes for a penny and jam crust for a further penny.

In the Second World War, food rationing was introduced just a few months after the war began and, once again, the housewife was left in no doubt of the role she was to play in the conflict. Advice came from government departments, local authorities, newspapers and magazines. In 1943 a Domestic

SERVICE ROOM, CORPORATION ST. RESTAURANT.

One of Coventry's Second World War British Restaurants. By 1944 the service was providing 82,600 meals across the city. Coventry Civic Restaurants Annual Reports 1951-64. *Courtesy of Coventry History Centre*

Front Exhibition was held at St Mary's Hall and women were urged to attend to gain instruction and knowledge in the latest Make Do and Mend Methods, to learn more about fuel economy from the Gas and Electricity stalls and find out how to tackle wartime cookery problems, plus 'a hundred different ways to conserve your coupons'. There was an exhibition of the work of domestic economy students from the Technical College, including rugs made from old stockings and felt hats, lamp shades from silk dresses, shoe trees from pegs and newspapers.

One of my favourite and most human of the 'Keep Calm and Carry On' stories is from Dorothy Parker who lived in Coundon with her husband and young daughter. To encourage jam making, there were extra sugar rations in the autumn but Dorothy dropped her 2lb bag of sugar on the garden path. The

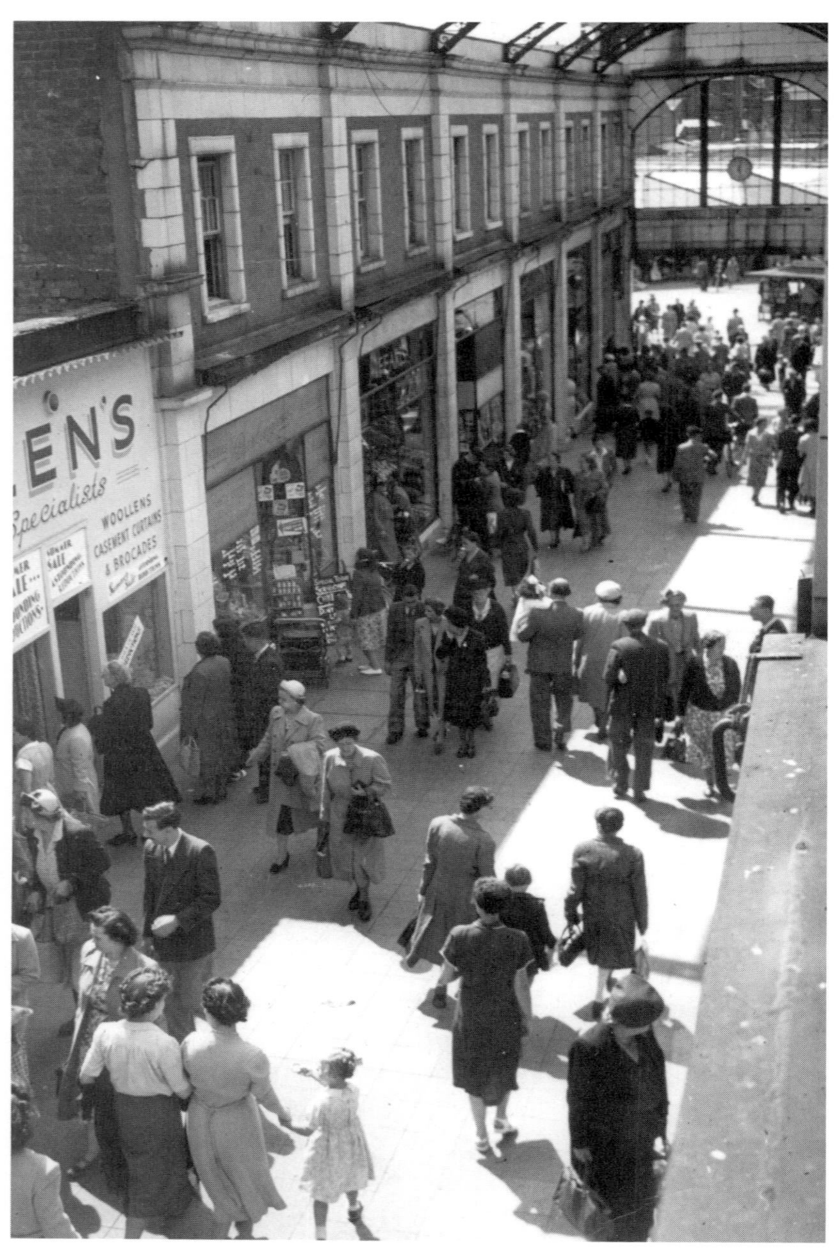

Shopping in the Arcade in the years after the Second World War. Only the steel structure of the roof remains but a new city centre is on its way. *Courtesy of Coventry History Centre*

bag split and the sugar went everywhere – 'I was so cross, but I swept it all up, dust and all, and made my jam as planned'.

The city's Emergency Committee began to serve meals after the November Blitz of 1940 and as the service grew, more premises in various parts of the city were found, under the authority of the British Restaurant Committee. When the war ended, the City Council took over the running of several of the restaurants, a mixture of service and self-service, providing breakfast, lunch, high tea and light refreshments. By the early 1950s, however, it was clear that the future of municipal restaurants was far from rosy, particularly in light of growing competition from private cafes and restaurants.

Despite continued rationing after the war, there was, among the wide scale plans to rebuild Coventry, a great deal of interest in what *Illustrated Magazine* called in 1949, 'the unique architectural experiment, known as the Shopping Precinct, which is to occupy the central position in Coventry'. The traffic free space where shops, restaurants and cafes were to face each other across formal gardens where children could be left safely to play while mothers shopped under the protection of arcades and canopies was referred to as a 'stark piece of functional architecture, streamlined and clean-looking, and perfectly in tune with a city that can make piston rods and aeroplane engines'. If she had heeded that pre-war advice in *the Midland Daily Telegraph*, and turned shopping into an adventure and a challenge to her knowledge, the savvy Coventry woman could look ahead to wonderful days of shopping. After all, the paper stressed, searching out the best brands, materials and choices was not just an interesting part of the housewife's job but an attractive hobby.

CHAPTER FOUR

Health and Welfare

Sickness and disease are no respecters of class, and during our hundred-year period, illnesses, including those now either eradicated or controlled, devastated the lives of individuals and their families, whatever their social status or income. But, before the Appointed Day of 5 July 1948, when the National Health Service began its provision of medical treatment free for all at the point of delivery, the treatment and attention that patients received depended a great deal on how much money they had. It was expensive to see a doctor and without cash or some form of medical insurance, many people soldiered on until their ill health became chronic or life threatening, ending their days in the workhouse infirmary or municipal hospital.

Between 1850 and 1950 there were vast improvements in public health, along with access to safer, purer water and foodstuffs. In towns and cities Medical Officers of Health developed and oversaw plans to tackle the ill effects of poor sanitation, overcrowding and bad housing, to reduce infant mortality rates and look after the youngest generation, upon whom the nation's future rested. Childbirth became safer and families got smaller but the extent to which women had neglected their own health did not become fully apparent until 1948, when, under the NHS Act, they began to be treated for illnesses and conditions that they had put up with for years, brushed aside as 'women's trouble', part and parcel of marriage, multiple pregnancies and raising a family. Women had put up and shut up for far too long.

The Home Nursing Service, 1950: The Morning Round Commences. Annual Report Coventry Medical Officer of Health, 1950. *Courtesy of Coventry History Centre*

As the nation began to develop the bare bones of a welfare state from the early twentieth century, the need to keep working men fit and well was undoubtedly at its core. The 1911 National Insurance Act introduced medical insurance designed to get sick men back to work as soon as possible but it did not cover their families. It was of course a disaster if accident or illness hit a husband and father when he was the main breadwinner, but families suffered in untold ways when mothers were laid low. In the early nineteenth century, Joseph Gutteridge's mother was crippled by rheumatic fever and her sons, 'after a fashion', did what they could under her instruction to keep the house in order. But when she died and a housekeeper was employed to look after them, they 'sadly missed the tender care and solicitude which only a mother can exhibit towards her children'.

Women were responsible for the welfare of the entire family; it was common for working-class women to go without so that their husbands could go to work with a full belly. The remaining food was divided among the children, with the mother making do with what was left – often the least nourishing. This pattern continued, even when she was pregnant or nursing an infant, and she became malnourished, weak and prone to illness.

Many a wife looked on with anxiety while her weekly accounts were scrutinised by a husband whose understanding of prices and budgeting was extremely limited. Many more women managed to conceal the ways in which they went without in order to feed their families and they weren't always those on the smallest incomes; during the Second World War, Evelyn Jones, mother and worker, fed her children before her husband came home, telling them she would eat later with him. When he came in, he thought she had eaten earlier with the children, although in fact she had just made do with whatever was left over. After the war she became very anaemic. Lack of good food, too little rest, combined with work, shopping, feeding and cleaning exhausted many women, many of whom looked older than their years.

Health Care Before the NHS

For much of the period, those who could afford it were treated in their own homes by a city doctor. Sometimes it was necessary to hire a sick nurse for a period of time, followed by convalescence at one of the seaside or spa resorts that grew in popularity during the nineteenth century. Among those most likely to receive such care were the families of manufacturers and professionals, living in the city's most spacious houses, with sufficient income to pay not just for medical attention but for the comforts that went some way to promoting healing and preventing permanent invalidity.

In the nineteenth century, hospital care for the rest of the city was mixed. The very poor had little choice but to rely on the workhouse when serious illness struck. Its first hospital buildings were small, with little attention paid to sanitation and ventilation, and patients – suffering from a range of problems

THE PUBLIC MEDICAL SERVICE

Medical Staff	*Hours of Consultation*		
	Morning	*Evening*	*Except*
Dr. BRAIN, 171, Gulson Road	9—10	6—7	Friday evgs.
and			
„ FROST, 298, Tile Hill Lane	9—10	6—7	Wednesday „
„ CATTO, 7 Eaton Road	8.45—9.45	6—7	Thur. & Sat. „
„ CLARK, 457 Foleshill Road	9—9.45	6—7	Thursday „
„ COGHILL, 26 Queens Road	9—9.45	5.30—7	Thursday „
„ COLLINGTON 147, Moseley Av.	9—10	6—7	Wednesday „
„ DABBS, 115 Holyhead Road	9—10	5.30—7	
„ ELFORD, Allesley Old Road	8.45—9.30	5.30—7	Thursday „
and			
„ SILKE, 271, Tile Hill Lane	10—10.30	7.30—8	Wednesday „
„ HOLMES			
60 Stoney Stanton Road	9—10	6—7.30	Thursday „
49 Engleton Road	11	6—6.45	Thursday „
„ HUGHES, 63, Woodside Avenue	9—9.30	7—8	Saturday „
„ KENDERDINE, 19 Queens Rd	9—9.45	5.30—7	
„ ERIC KENDERDINE, 49 Earlsdon Av		4.30—6.30	
„ LAVERTY, 15 Queens Road	9—9.45	6—7	Thursday „
„ LOWE 148 Kensington Road	9—10	5—7	Thursday „
355 Tile Hill Lane	10.45—11	7.30—8	Thursday „
„ MACQUAIDE & SHEPHERD			
108 Cox Street	9—10 2—3	6—7	Thursday „
„ MOISER, 34 Holyhead Road	9—9.30	6—7	Saturday „
„ R. L. MOISER, 403, Walsgrave Rd.	9—10	6—7	Thursday „
„ SHULMAN, 57 Walsgrave Rd	9—10	5.30—7	Thursday „
„ SODEN, Queen Victoria Road	9—10	6—7.30	Wednesday „
„ TURNER, Moseley Avenue	9—10	6—7	Thursday „
and			
„ GREGG, 270, Holyhead Road	9-30—10-30	7—8	Wednesday „
„ VAUGHAN, 56, Binley Rd	9—10	2—3	Thursday „
49 Walsgrave Rd.	9—10	5—7	Thursday „
93 Ansty Rd.	2—3	6—7	Wednesdays „
„ WEARING, Eaton Road	9—9.45	6—7	Thursday „
„ WILL Arran House Binley Rd	9—9.45	6—7.30	Wed. „

All Messages to be left before 10 a.m. otherwise the usual visiting fees will be charged.

Dr....

Supervisors and Auditors : **LEECH, EVANS & CO.,** CHARTERED ACCOUNTANTS.

DARLASTON HOUSE, WARWICK ROAD,
(Corner St. Patricks Road) **COVENTRY.**

WHERE SUBSCRIPTIONS MAY BE LEFT.

Change of residence must be notified either to collector or to office as above.

Medical Card from the 1930s, showing doctors participating in the Coventry Public Medical Service. *Courtesy of David Fry*

MEMBERS IN ARREAR ARE NOT ENTITLED TO BENEFIT.

The Coventry Public Medical Service
The Coventry New Dispensary
Medical Aid Clubs.

It has been decided by all the medical practitioners engaged in the above practices that the following scale of charges shall come into operation from October 1st, 1937, viz: –

First patient	- -	4d. a week.
Second "	- -	4d. a week.
Third "	- -	2d. a week.
Fourth "	- -	2d. a week.

Extra children over a total of four members in the same family, free of charge.

Those members who are now old age pensioners will only be charged the present rate of 3d. a week.

The benefits of this Service are intended for those whose average weekly earnings do not exceed 80/-, and the Committee reserves to itself the right of terminating the contract at any time.

The same Medical Card, showing scale of charges for the Coventry New Dispensary Medical Aid Clubs. *Courtesy of David Fry*

including infectious diseases and mental illness – were often nursed by female workhouse inmates. Improvements came towards the end of the century; a new infirmary was begun in 1889 and certified nurses were sought via the Workhouse Nursing Associations in Manchester and London as well as probationer nurses and night attendants. In the 1890s, Poor Law Guardian Amy Hurlston managed to persuade the Board to hire its first night nurse for the infirmary. By 1901 Mrs Sarah Dodd was employed as the workhouse superintendent sick nurse and five sick nurses were with her on census day.

From the 1830s Coventry had a General (Charitable) Dispensary, which, with the Coventry and Warwickshire Hospital, offered free treatment to those who had no other means of receiving help but were nonetheless regarded, in the Victorian spirit of the day, as being 'deserving' or 'respectable' poor, as opposed to the destitute directed to the workhouse infirmary. It relied on contributions and subscriptions to continue its work and began life in Little

Coventry and Warwickshire Hospital Outpatient Department, opened in 1910. *Courtesy of David Fry*

Park Street, moving to a site in Stoney Stanton Road, officially opened in 1867, providing sixty beds.

Those who could afford to do so joined the Provident Dispensary, also sustained by charitable donation but applying another favourite Victorian principle – that of 'self-help'. For a weekly sum, members received medical assistance and treatment from the dispensary in Bayley Lane. Paying into such schemes – some of which affiliated with the Provident – was how many families sought to cover the cost of medicines and seeing a doctor, but regular payments relied on regular work and faced with a reduced and limited weekly income, it was easy to let insurance payments slip in order to feed and clothe the family. When young Grace Charlton (from *Hurdy Gurdy Days*) became ill with a high temperature and sore throat, her mother was immediately worried because her dispensary club payment of 4*d* a week was in arrears and a doctor, if needed, might refuse to come. Her Sunday-best shoes went straight to the pawnshop, raising 8*d* to take to the dispensary. It was still not enough to clear the debt but it did ensure that the doctor attended Grace (although he looked first at the family's dispensary payment book before examining the patient) and when he diagnosed diphtheria, there was another dash to the pawnshop, this time with bedding to get the five shillings (a significant sum, given that the family's weekly rent was three and a half shillings) needed for medicine, not included in the dispensary's cover. More anxiety followed when Grace could not open her mouth to let her mother treat her throat with the life-saving medicine. It was not the doctor who came to her rescue but one of the District Nurses who lived together in a house nearby and whose swift response saved Grace's life. She belonged to the Coventry District Nursing Association, based in The Quadrant, whose income was derived solely from box collections, sales of work, jumble sales and donations from patients, with no help at all given from hospital funds. By 1915 a team of four nurses was headed by Superintendent Miss Crabb

Coventry and Warwickshire Hospital Residential Staff, 1913. *Courtesy of Coventry History Centre*

Christmas time on the Gulson Ward for children, Coventry and Warwickshire Hospital. The ward was opened in 1874 after £4000 was raised by Mrs John Gulson. *Courtesy of David Fry*

and their 'kindness and wholehearted services' had earned them praise from across the city; industrialist J.K. Starley and his wife showed their appreciation by sending the nurses the gift of a bicycle, so valuable for their work. In that year, they made nearly 15,000 free of charge visits to patients and were hoping that their summer flag day would bring in enough for them to continue to help the city's poorest folk.

Coventry and Warwickshire Hospital grew as a result of bequests and income derived from the Hospital Saturday Fund. Additional beds were provided for wounded soldiers during the First World War, by which time there was also an isolation hospital on Stoney Stanton Road for fever cases and a smallpox hospital at Pinley. In 1929 the Workhouse Infirmary transferred into Corporation hands (becoming Gulson Hospital) and a new fever hospital, with Council funding, opened at Whitley in 1934. It was not until after the Second World War that numbers of infectious diseases began to diminish, thanks to the success of mass vaccination programmes, and the need for separate fever hospitals decreased.

Public Health Challenges

One of the greatest challenges faced by women bringing up families in the city was the battle against disease fought continuously in the poorest of districts with their attendant evils of dilapidated buildings, overcrowding and poor sanitation. A very unflattering picture of the city centre was painted by an architectural journal, *The Builder*, in May 1862, showing how,

> Sedulously every corner of garden-ground, orchards, and other vacant spaces must have been built upon. The courts are provided with public privies and monster ash-pits which, when emptied, deal disease around among the occupiers of the crowded confines. In [just] this one street we have an accumulation of the principal sanitary errors, the cesspool system, overcrowding, and bad damp and filth absorbing pebble paving.

The report acknowledged that improvements had been made by the Board of Health, established in Coventry in 1849, including a sewerage scheme. An artesian well and reservoir in Spon End were built and water mains were laid, supplying, by 1851, just under half of the city's properties. With safer water, the death rate fell from twenty-seven to twenty-three per thousand in the 1850s and a fulltime inspector was appointed to deal with privies and cesspits, yet *The Builder* still considered supervision to be 'feeble' in some places, with 'the cesspool system remain[ing] in triumphant possession of a great portion of the town'.

In the 1930s, cobbled lanes near Broadgate were cleared away in order to construct Trinity Street. I have many times heard the lament over the council's alleged short-sightedness in demolishing the fine medieval buildings that lined these lanes, yet this description from *The Builder* alerts me to a different picture;

Court number Two, White Friars Lane, closed in 1911 and a demolition order made in 1912. Annual Report Coventry Medical Officer of Health, 1911. *Courtesy of Coventry History Centre*

> In the heart of the city, close to the opulent market-place, under the shadow of two magnificent churches, and in the immediate neighbourhood of Priory-row, the butchers congregate, and slaughtering goes on in the public thoroughfare. As we passed, a sheep was slaughtered in this public way. A greasy bucket was held to receive the blood, which in time overflowed and escaped down the steep gutter of the row, in company with paunch stuff and other offal – a most revolting arrangement. The houses, once picturesque and clean, were pleasant residences when few people lived in each of them, and there was plenty of air from gardens in the rear, but, converted into butchers' shops and offices, into cramped additions, and with living rooms excavated below them, they certainly form but a sorry substitute for a meat market.

Unsurprisingly, reaction from the Coventry press to this slur on the city's good name was indignant; *The Builder* apologised – its intention, it insisted, was not to cause offence but to point the way to improvement and it explained its continued commitment to 'calling for homes, not lairs, for the honest workers in our land'. Not surprising, then, that those who could afford to do so moved out of the central area as, slowly, land around the city became available for development.

Too often poor housing goes hand-in-hand with low and irregular wages and families needed more than a little good fortune to break out of the cycle of poverty that shortened their life expectancy and made daily life such a struggle. John Prest, who wrote about Coventry in the Industrial Revolution, measured living standards among weavers using 'the good old nineteenth century yardstick':

> If an artisan could afford no bacon, he was badly off. If he could afford bacon, but no meat, then he was doing middling well. If he could afford butcher's meat, and had a clock in the house, then he was very well off indeed.

When trade was good, the weaving family's diet was more varied, but in lean times, the most nutritious foods were cut back or eliminated and the amount of bread and potatoes increased, keeping bellies as full as possible but not providing the building blocks to future health.

There were also occupational hazards to deal with; weaving was regarded as an unhealthy trade, the weaver hunched over the loom, often working in the cold with the windows shut, because smoke from the fire could damage the silk, and circulating air could alter its moisture content. Because of the high rates of respiratory disease in the city centre, one of the most important lifelines for the weaving family was occasional access to the countryside that hemmed in the city. The Gutteridge family's house up a back yard at the far end of Gosford Street overlooked the workhouse but also had a 'glorious and extensive view of fields', a vision that, perhaps, offered as much hope as it induced fear. Some businessmen in Coventry, including Charles Bray and the Cash brothers, recognised the benefits not just of workers visiting the countryside but of having their own land to cultivate, which could be used to get weavers through periods of unemployment and thereby retain their independence as well as their family's health. To this end, a number of allotments were acquired and some manufacturers promoted the idea of the cottage factory as an alternative to the large factories so hated by the artisan weavers. A row of houses was connected to an engine house which supplied the looms in each house with steam power, and each house had a garden large enough to grow vegetables. It is still possible to see those built by Cash's in the 1850s alongside the canal on Cash's Lane off Foleshill Road.

The experiment barely had time to begin before the ribbon industry was plunged into a devastating depression from which it never fully recovered and so it is impossible to measure its success but it is fair to say that allotment cultivation has been of enormous help to thousands of families. *Hurdy Gurdy Days* refers to the outskirts of early twentieth century Coventry as being full of allotments, where 'it was a common sight to see [men] trundling their little trucks along the street full of

Surviving example of a cottage factory, Cash's Lane, an attempt in the 1850s to combine the advantages of factory production with the traditions of home working. Power was supplied to the topshops via an engine house and workers were supplied with decent sized gardens promoting the growth of vegetables and healthy living conditions. *Author's own collection*

Coventry City Libraries' Second World War exhibition advertising its resources to help those growing their own vegetables and keeping small livestock. *Courtesy of Coventry History Centre*

vegetables and flowers'. In 1917 the *Midland Daily Telegraph* calculated that there were around 4,000 allotment holders in Coventry, helping to combat food shortages. During the Second World War when land was made available to 'dig for victory', Dorothy Parker, who we met in Chapter Three, living in Coundon, had an allotment at the bottom of her garden where the family grew most of its vegetables and kept hens.

Childbirth

In 1924 the Workers' Birth Control Group claimed that it was four times more dangerous to bear a child than to work in a coal mine. Given that that there was no trade more dangerous than mining, this was a sobering statistic. Despite the insanitary conditions affecting much of the poorest housing, it was still regarded as safer to deliver a baby at home than in hospital where

Woman and Child, 1900. *Courtesy of Coventry History Centre*

infection could, and did, spiral out of control, killing wards full of mothers and their babies. By the late nineteenth century it was fashionable for those who could afford it to be attended to and delivered by a doctor, but the majority of women laboured with the help of a trusted midwife. One Coventry woman, born in 1914, remembered that there was a very good midwife who lived opposite them, delivering all her mother's babies from her onwards (there were, in all, eight children and one stillbirth).

How much help a woman received, who it came from and for how long was entirely dependent on what she could afford. As we have seen, those who could, paid into the Provident, but extra payments were required for attendance in childbirth. The 1911 National Insurance Act included a thirty shillings maternity benefit payable to the wives of insured men and this did allow some women to employ a midwife for their labour, with enough perhaps – if all went smoothly – for a little help with domestic chores or childcare for a day or so afterwards. Before then – and afterwards for many women – pregnancy was a time of intense anxiety, when women hoped above all to avoid sickness and any complications that would require a doctor or a hospital stay. Many relied on the help of neighbours to rally round until the new mother was fit enough to get out of bed and resume her duties. In order not to incur further fees, women commonly ignored resulting problems such as tears, prolapsed wombs or varicose veins. Coventry had two lying-in charities to offer free midwife care for pregnant women, tickets for groceries and the loan of bags of baby linen but, in the spirit of the Provident, these were reserved solely for the wives of those regarded to be poor but 'deserving mechanics and labourers'.

In the nineteenth century, as we saw in the last chapter, unmarried mothers with no family or friends to offer help had little choice but to turn to the workhouse for confinement and shelter where they were often harshly dealt with and made fully aware of their shameful condition. As the century wore on, there were some stirrings of pity towards girls who it was considered had been wronged; in 1897 the Guardians asked the police to begin criminal proceedings against the man responsible for having 'immoral connection' with a young girl – possibly under the age of 16 – who came into the workhouse to give birth to her illegitimate child. Although the man was not prosecuted, the Guardians took out a summons against him demanding explanation as to why he had not contributed to the upkeep of the baby.

The majority of midwives in the nineteenth century received little or no formal training but instead learned on the job, many trusted by local doctors to work independently, calling for assistance when it was required. Coventry is lucky to have the preserved registers of Mary Eaves, a midwife living and practicing in Spon End from around 1847 to 1875. Like most midwives, she was married with children of her own, living among the women she helped. Married women and widows might be solely occupied in this way or they might combine midwifery with another trade, supplementing their income when times were hard. Yet, despite the many trusted relationships that existed between doctors and midwives, there was also a great deal of disquiet about the quality of care that some self-proclaimed midwives gave. In *Martin Chuzzlewit* (1844), Charles Dickens created the character of Sarah Gamp, a name that became a by-word for a careless, ignorant and dirty Victorian midwife. There may have been such women in Coventry but there were many more providing a dependable, affordable and invaluable service to women who had no choice but to put all their faith in their years of experience.

In 1902 the Midwives' Act was passed, coming into force in 1905 and specifying that from 1910, only trained 'certified' midwives or those recognised and trusted by local doctors would be allowed to continue to practice. Charges of malpractice, negligence and misconduct were to be investigated by local authorities and failure to register while practicing could lead to a court summons and fine. Of the twenty midwives certified in Coventry in 1906, seven had received some training and all were visited by the Medical Officer of Health who regularly inspected their bags and registers. By 1911 he reported his satisfaction that midwives were paying more attention to the cleanliness of their bags and appliances than formerly. That year, midwives attended 2,309 births, of which just 123 were labelled 'doctors' cases'. By the Second World War, local authorities were not just registering midwives, they were required to employ them, providing them with uniforms and necessary equipment.

Harriet Louisa Ives began work as a district midwife in Coventry in the early twentieth century, having trained at Birmingham Maternity Hospital. According to her obituary in the local press in 1952, she was the city's first trained midwife. She calculated that by the time her career ended after the Second World War, she had brought 7,000 babies into the world, as well as training midwives at the city's hospitals. Nurse Ives was deeply involved in community work, including the movement to establish local infant welfare centres throughout the city.

During the Second World War pregnant women were supposed to be evacuated from the city. Mona Jones was taken to Shipston-on-Stour to stay, with other expectant mothers, in the wing of a large house where they were required to clean, meaning that the lady of the house 'got free servants'.

Gulson Hospital – New Nurses Home, 1930, Annual Report Coventry Medical Officer of Health, 1930. *Courtesy of Coventry History Centre*

Imagine us, she wrote, 'crowded round the attic windows, sobbing our socks off, looking at the bright red sky, knowing our city was being bombed'. No small wonder, then, that many women gravitated back home, preferring to be in their own surroundings even if that meant putting the midwifery service under additional strain. District midwives delivered babies at home with emergency cases admitted to Gulson Hospital with the mothers subsequently evacuated to small midwifery homes across Warwickshire.

The NHS Act brought enormous relief to expectant mothers at not having to budget and save for medical support. In her wonderful account of maternity care before the NHS, Janet Frances Smith includes the story of Joan who was taken to Gulson Hospital in 1937 with a threatened miscarriage. By the time she left the hospital weeks later with her healthy baby boy, she faced a hospital bill for £35, an impossible amount to pay back. When her husband then lost his job, the amount was dropped to £1, which they paid back at a shilling a week, but even this was difficult to do during such hard times. After 1948, as well as free care, there was much better coordination between midwives, clinics and family doctors, with clear information for women about where to go and how to book in. The district midwife, however, remained at the very heart of women's care, using good local knowledge to work well with a whole range of services to ensure a better quality of life for her patients, liaising with landlords, housing officers, nurses and health visitors. Local authorities provided (and paid for) additional training opportunities and refresher courses which private midwives would previously have had to pay for themselves.

Bringing up the Family

In the nineteenth century, despite the overall drop in the death rate after improvements to the water supply and sanitation, the death rates in some of the city's wards remained alarmingly high. To take one year at random – 1889 – the Medical Officer of Health reported that the city's infant mortality rate was eight times higher than the general death rate, with deaths of infants under the age of 1 accounting for over a quarter of all deaths in several districts. A fifth of the infant deaths were registered as due to prematurity. Families battled with chest ailments, scarlet fever, typhoid, diphtheria, whooping cough and infant diarrhoea. The Medical Officer noted that there had been six measles epidemics in the last ten years, causing 160 deaths. As the disease could be contracted from someone who was showing no indication of it, his comment that measles struck within 'the most intelligent and observing classes' as well as the children of 'poorer and less careful parents' because children were unwittingly sent to school when they were infectious, serves to remind us of the harsh judgements directed at the poor, despite their best efforts to care for their children.

The Medical Officer had the power to close schools in order to contain epidemics; the Wheatley Street School log-book for November 1896 records the absence of many girls owing to illnesses in their homes, including measles, scarlet fever and diphtheria and two days later the school was required to close. When it opened over three weeks later, all staff were present but pupil attendance was poor, as many girls were still unwell. New cases of scarlet fever and measles continued to be reported into the following year. A Chauntry Place resident remembered his house being turned pink by distemper following an outbreak of scarlet fever in the family. Fumigation and the disinfection of bedding and clothing was the responsibility of the Medical Officer of Health but although this might deal with the immediate effects of infection, overcrowding, the impossibility of through ventilation in so many houses, along with the frequent blocking of drains that led to so called 'filth diseases' made the task of providing safer public health in some parts of the city very difficult. In 1889 the Medical Officer of Health, Dr Snell, concluded, wistfully, that

> The erection of artisans' dwellings, either as houses or larger sets of buildings…would be a great blessing to the poor of the district … and a far more useful object for philanthropy than the expenditure of money in adding to the already too numerous charitable doles of the City.

One Coventry woman, born in Henry Street (between Leicester Street and Cook Street) before the First World War, recalled that when she contracted scarlet fever, aged 5, she was sent to Coventry and Warwickshire Hospital because the area where she lived was too congested for her to be treated at home. Her younger sister's death from dysentery, at just 13 months old, may well have been caused by the insanitary conditions of the district. Diarrhoea was an extremely dangerous condition; in 1900, for example, it was responsible for more infant deaths than any other illness, and of the seventy-five lives that it took that year, the majority were babies under the age of one. Summer was the most difficult time to control the conditions that caused diarrhoea, particularly for mothers who bottle-fed their babies in homes where keeping baby milk and foods cool and free from bacteria was extremely difficult. A long hot, dry spell in the summer of 1898 had pushed Coventry's infant mortality rate above the national average in that year. In his 1900 Report, the Medical Officer highlighted that of sixty-eight babies who died between July and the end of October, fifty-six were bottle fed. He outlined some of the dangers facing young children exposed to 'wrongly directed artificial feeding', including the too early administration of starchy foods and 'ill-devised "infants' foods"', not to mention the use of dirty bottles and unclean receptacles for storing milk.

From time-to-time Coventry was also hit by outbreaks of smallpox, enough to strike terror into any parent's heart. Since the 1850s a series of Acts had made vaccination of young children compulsory, but a combination of fears over the safety of the vaccine, plus moral and religious objections to the use of calf lymph as opposed to human lymph in the vaccine, and opposition to the notion of compulsion had resulted in a very strong anti-vaccination movement. A large demonstration was held in Coventry in August 1891 to greet the return of a man who had spent fourteen days in prison for refusing to have his child vaccinated and the numbers of those defying the Poor Law Guardians, whose job it was to oversee vaccinations, grew to the extent that by 1895 take up was just four per cent, whereas in 1889 it had been ninety-six per cent. By 1896 there were over 7,000 children under the age of 10 who were not vaccinated and in that year, smallpox returned to the city. A number of cycle workers had gone out to Lisbon to work in a factory and on return, one of them, along with his wife, was found to be infected and sent to the isolation hospital. The Medical Officer wanted to vaccinate and therefore protect fifty poorly children already in the hospital but, even faced with the prospect of their children contracting smallpox, the parents of only one child consented. In 1897 the city built a special smallpox hospital in Pinley in an attempt to reduce the risks of spreading the disease among those patients in the Stoney Stanton Road isolation hospital. The smallpox hospital was kept in constant readiness to admit patients and had its own steam disinfector on the premises. A

Exterior of Smallpox Tents, Pinley Hospital, 1903. Annual Report Coventry Medical Officer of Health, 1903. *Courtesy of Coventry History Centre*

change in the law in 1898 allowed those with 'conscientious' objections to refuse vaccination for their children but for others, attempts were made to make things easier for families by vaccinating in the home rather than at vaccination stations at particular hours. Despite the substitution of human for calf lymph, Coventry's take up of the vaccination remained low, with just twenty-two per cent of children vaccinated in 1930.

Feeding Baby

By 1904, a leaflet on infant feeding was delivered to all Coventry houses where a birth had occurred. In the early 1900s, the health of the British population was a cause for serious concern. Recruitment for the Boer War had brought to light the fact that thousands of young working class men, essential to the task of maintaining the Empire and working in industry, were in fact too sickly and weak to do so. Medical officers knew only too well that in order to reduce rates of infant mortality, there must be vast improvements in living conditions. In the absence of funds for immediate and vast rebuilding projects, however, they worked within communities and sought to instruct working-class women on how to raise the children who would then be fit enough to protect Britain's position in the world. It was hard to do so without appearing to apportion blame; there were concerns that too many mothers were being badly advised on infant feeding by well-meaning grandmothers or neighbours. Dr Snell's infant feeding leaflet advised mothers – 'if the breast milk is sufficient in quantity' – to feed baby every two hours during the day and every four hours at night for the first three months, with the intervals between feeds lengthening until at six months, other foods could be introduced. Breastfeeding should be stopped by nine months because by then the milk was poor, with insufficient nourishment for the child and with the risk that the mother would become weak and more liable to various illnesses. Regular feeding and regular amounts of milk (the latter being extremely difficult to monitor) would prevent indigestion, flatulence and wind and putting the baby to the breast merely to keep it quiet would have the opposite effect.

The salient point was of course 'if breast milk is sufficient'. In the second half of the nineteenth century, middle-class mothers became less likely to employ wet nurses and instead – if possible – to feed their own infants. Many were well supported by medical attendants, a nanny, a maid and a cook, with rest and nutritious food assured. In such circumstances, breastfeeding was given the best chance to get established. For women living in poor and overcrowded housing, there was less chance of success. Mothers were only too aware of the benefits of breast feeding; it was safest for baby, it was cheaper than substitute baby foods and many hoped that it might prevent another pregnancy occurring too soon, as prolonged feeding was widely regarded as contraceptive. Yet there were so many obstacles – malnourishment in pregnancy and afterwards, caused by putting husband and children first, continuing paid work and housework right up to delivery and then resumed before proper strength was regained, low birth weight babies who struggled to feed, hungry babies who were never satisfied. A collection of letters published in 1915 by the Women's Co-operative Guild, campaigning for improvements in care for mothers and babies, provide moving and harrowing accounts of some of the challenges women faced. This woman's words say a great deal;

> Through my married life I have had a good, kind partner, which means so much to the wife, and who always provided me with a doctor and a good nurse for my confinements, which goes without saying that the mother and child have a much better chance than other neglected ones. The first five were born with fifteen months between; then there was a wait of eight years for the sixth, and three years for the seventh. I have always worked hard both before and after childbirth. Give a woman a quiet home and an easy conscience and good plain food and I see no reason why both mother and child should not do well.

Dr Snell's leaflet advised Coventry mothers that the best substitute for breast milk was fresh cow's milk; milk-fed children, he noted, had clear skin and good colour, harder bones and stronger teeth than those reared on other infant foods. A tablespoon of milk should be diluted with water, to which a half of teaspoon of Demerara sugar should be added. As the infant grew, less water was needed but, if possible, two teaspoons of cream should be mixed in until, by six months, pure milk (always boiled) could be taken. The advice was accompanied by instructions on how to store the milk (in a clean jug placed in a saucepan of cold water on the stove) and how to give it to baby – preferably in a boat shaped bottle with an opening at each end, as opposed to one with a long tube – and how to clean the bottle (in a bowl containing washing soda, with the teat in a separate cup without the soda). By the last few decades of the nineteenth century, better off women who bottle-fed their infants had a reasonable chance of doing so safely, following advice on hygiene and sterilisation and doing so in houses in which it was easier to keep milk cool and free from bacteria. But still the highest number of infant deaths from diarrhoea occurred in the smallest houses where keeping foodstuffs cool during hot spells was almost impossible.

Just as mothers knew of the benefits of breast milk, they understood the importance of pure cow's milk but for many, this was prohibitively expensive, and despite the cost, could not be guaranteed to be safe, given the dilapidated state of some city shops (not to mention the unhygienic conditions in some local milking sheds). In 1900 ten per cent of milk samples collected by public health officials were found to be adulterated and in addition, milk was not always properly covered in shops. Many families relied instead on tinned milk, not just for baby but to put in tea; by the end of the century, condensed milk was a popular choice, yet the cheaper the brand, the less nutritious this sugared milk was for infants.

There was also widespread and emotive advertising for baby foods, including dried milk and cereals, although in 1906, Coventry's first health visitor, warned of the 'poor little things' who were becoming objects for experiment, being given all kinds of 'doubtful foods' leading to the formation of unhealthy eating habits. In 1917 an advertisement in the *Midland Daily Telegraph* warned mothers that it was recently stated that it was more dangerous to be a baby in England than a soldier in France and urged them to rely on a supplement called Chymol which added 'vital life elements' destroyed in boiling and cooking. It could be added to milk, taken on a spoon or spread on bread, enabling baby to digest food, keep it down and thrive.

As early as 1900, Coventry's Medical Officer believed that there was much to be said for experiments being carried out in some British towns to provide a municipal supply of sterilised milk in small, clean, stoppered bottles. It was not in fact until the First World War that the government issued a free milk order; in Coventry, mothers could attend voluntary infant welfare centres in Lord Street, Leicester Causeway and at the Stoke Parish

SIX DON'TS FOR BABY

Don't from his skin the glorious sun exclude.

Don't "hush" and rock him when in fractious mood.

Don't let him feed except at stated times.

Don't overclothe or cramp his growing limbs.

Don't pick him up whenever by chance he cries,

Remember best he grows as still he lies.

And e'en before his lips can murmur "Mummy"

Don't let him suck the unhygienic dummy.

Six Don'ts for Baby, Coventry Health Department, 1935 Local Notes from Better Health, 1929-40. *Courtesy of Coventry History Centre*

Rooms and participate in a scheme to provide their babies with a pure milk supply. It was stated that no mother who applied would be refused and in addition, advice on feeding, exercise and cleanliness was given.

Mothers and Babies

The Maternity and Child Welfare Act of 1918 enabled local authorities to provide a range of services for mothers and their children. Just after the First World War, Coventry's team of health visitors were visiting new mothers, often greeted, according to Miss Barratt, the Superintendent Health Visitor, with, 'I'm so glad you have called; I hoped you would be coming soon', issuing advice on feeding and invitations to the newly established Welfare Centre at the Council House, open three afternoons a week, thus building on the foundations established by voluntary pressure groups such as the Care of Maternity

Coventry Municipal Welfare Centre: The Infant Weighing Room, Barracks Square, 1925. Annual Report Coventry Medical Officer of Health, 1925. *Courtesy of Coventry History Centre*

Committee, which had opened a baby clinic in the city centre in 1915. Here, a district nurse and a local doctor offered advice on weight, diet and baby management and the following year, the Committee had opened 'Dunsmoor' on Holyhead Road as a nursery for the children of mothers with husbands at the Front, with the promise that 'a high intelligence would preside over the important task of making [the children] grow into strong maturity'. While this facility was undoubtedly a boon for the few mothers lucky enough to get a place for their children – 'setting her free to work for the country' – the heaviest emphasis was placed on the welfare of the children. An appeal for funding stressed that 'never was there greater need to care for children, but often they are left in unskilled hands and in unhygienic surroundings to suffer many ways in consequence. The Nursery is a wartime effort to combat those risks'.

Similar thinking went into the idea of National Baby Weeks, held towards the end of the war, with Coventry's first one taking place in July 1918. National propaganda, with the slogan to 'Save every Saveable Child', stressed the need to 'form an army to fight the foes of ignorance, indifference and neglect' and Coventry's event was similar to those staged in other towns and cities, including exhibitions of baby equipment, practical advice and competitions for the healthiest babies, with impressive prizes; the first prize in Coventry was a pram donated by Messrs Dunkley's Ltd in Birmingham, where manufacture was carried out by one-armed, discharged soldiers.

Mothers could be in little doubt that the work of rearing the next generation, particularly at a time of national crisis was considered to be of enormous national importance. After the war, health visiting, the sale of safe, wholesome milk, food and supplements at clinics, alongside feeding advice all contributed to falling infant mortality rates. In 1923 the welfare clinics distributed over nine tons of dried milk, two and half hundredweight of groats, 1,476 tins of Ovaltine and 168 pounds

Prize winners and decorated prams at a baby show held in the grounds of Foleshill House, Great Heath. *Coventry Graphic,* 30 July 1920. *Courtesy of Coventry History Centre*

HOUSEHOLD
HEALTH HINTS

Don't omit fresh fruit and green vegetables from your diet at this time of the year.

Keep your milk cool and covered.

Never allow tinned foods (after opening) to stand before eating.

Flies avoid yellow glass ; have the latter fitted in your larder.

Keep bedroom windows open day and night.

Do not place wet refuse in the dust-bin—burn it.

Take an interest in the sanitation of your home.

1930s Household Hints, Coventry Health Department, Local Notes from Better Health, 1929-40. *Courtesy of Coventry History Centre*

of cod liver oil and malt. Over four tons of the milk was provided to mothers free of charge. In 1931 the infant mortality rate in Coventry for babies under 1 year of age was 57.7 per 1,000 births (compared with a rate of 200 per 1,000 in 1898), whereas the rate for England and Wales was sixty-six per thousand and seventy per thousand in the largest towns. From 1930 a scheme of cooperation between the voluntary and Council run services operated in the city with ten infant centres by 1932, with the Public Health department supplying nursing staff.

In the inter-war years, however, clearly not enough was done to look after the country's mothers, for national maternal mortality rates actually rose. Although Coventry was an expanding city in the inter-war years, with its engineering industries paying relatively high wages in the 1930s, there was nonetheless a great deal of unemployment in the 1920s and in the aftermath of the 1929 Wall Street Crash. When families suffered, as a result of pay cuts, or refused benefits, it was often women who bore the brunt of the poverty, making sure the children were fed and that no one knew the extent of the deprivation endured. One woman recalled that if people called round to her house unexpectedly, her mother would rattle the plates in the pantry so that they would think that she was preparing a meal, disguising the fact that there was little or no food in the house. When the Poor Law was replaced by Public Assistance Committees and when families were granted relief in their homes (either as money or 'in kind', from Council run stores or by agreement with tradesmen) rather than having to go into the workhouse, the sense of shame felt in attending interviews for help during the infamous Means Test years was still hard to bear.

It is no wonder, then, that maternal mortality rates were slow to fall. Male unemployment was regarded as the biggest tragedy of these years, children were

GOOD MORNING!

A GOOD day must have a good beginning.

Summer or winter the window has, of course, been open so that you have been breathing pure air all night.

Night air is not different from day air. It may be *colder*, but the air outside the house is always *cleaner* than the air inside. You must let it into your room and into your lungs if you want to wake up fresh and fit for the day's work or play.

More household hints from Coventry Health Department, Local Notes from Better Health, 1929-40. *Courtesy of Coventry History Centre* beginning to benefit from improved welfare facilities, and the country was slow to wake up to the fact that expectant mothers needed more help. Coventry's Public Health Department responded to government directives to tackle this by providing twenty-one maternity beds at Gulson Hospital and urging women that 'the most valuable insurance against maternal risk is systematic ante-natal care', with more sessions at clinics laid on at Dunsmoor, Gulson Hospital and Sibree Hall on Warwick Road. By 1949 the maternal mortality rate was 0.8 per thousand births (compared with 0.98 nationally) and was, for the second year running, the lowest rate ever recorded in Coventry.

Family Planning

By 1950, contraception, although not openly discussed, was widely used. Not only were most families smaller than those produced by Victorian couples, it had become increasingly possible to plan one's family, rather than to produce babies for as long as fertility continued. This brought about enormous changes in women's quality of life and hopes for the future; by 1940 less than ten per cent of families in Britain had more than five children and increasingly, women went into marriage expecting to be able to limit the number of children that they had. Even in the 1950s, however, only married women could be advised at family planning clinics. Dr Janet Done, Coventry's Senior Medical Officer for Maternal and Child Welfare in the 1950s, frustrated at this limitation, was not alone in her determination to do what she could to help as many women access birth control as possible, even if it meant ignoring the lack of a wedding ring.

In the inter-war years, despite greater openness about birth control, many local authorities, including Coventry, continued to believe that contraception was a private matter between husband and wife and were unwilling to provide advice centres. In January 1930 birth control was debated in Coventry's Council Chamber, with Councillor Ellen Hughes arguing that as the wealthier classes had been paying for contraceptive advice for years, working-class women should also be given that information at a clinic. Surely, she said, it was preferable for a woman to have three children and rear them all, than to have twelve and bury nine. Another councillor stated his belief that the majority of couples were already practising some form of contraception but Councillor Hughes said that be that as it may, the real need was for scientific, informed knowledge. In 1930, it was more common for couples to rely on abstinence, withdrawal and abortion than on artificial methods such as sheaths, sponges or pessaries, none of which, of course, were free.

Women of means (or women who could discreetly get hold of some money in an emergency) could find a doctor or private clinic to perform an abortion when unwanted pregnancies occurred. The majority of working-class women sought either to end the pregnancy on their own, or with the help of a friend or family member. If all else failed, there would be a visit to a woman known in the neighbourhood to help out at such times of crisis. The dangers associated with backstreet abortions are well known but many home remedies could also end in disaster. Women forced themselves to fall down the stairs, to sit in scalding hot baths, drinking gin, to use knitting needles, or use potions made from lead, washing soda, quinine and tobacco, to name but a few.

In desperation they might turn to advertisements, such as one in the *Coventry Herald* in 1893, for Thomasso's 'Magic' Pills to correct all irregularities and 'Remove Obstruction' from any cause. The packaging and the message were ambiguous but women knew what was meant. The advert warned them to make sure they got the genuine brand, with the green label, which could be bought at chemists or posted from Westminster Bridge Road, London.

Old Age

Low wages, widowhood, ill health and lack of health care were among the reasons why saving for old age was out of the question for so many women. When Poor Law Guardian Amy Hurlston appeared before the Royal Commission on the Aged Poor in the 1890s, her evidence came from talking with women employed in various Midland industries. One cycle polisher saw 'no ultimate hope of evading the workhouse should she live to extreme old age', but as many industrial employers would not take on women over the age of 50, the workhouse could be the only sanctuary for those with no other means of managing and Miss Hurlston thought it very likely that a majority of them would become paupers. She found that women would try hard to keep up payments for sickness and burial clubs but found it impossible to save for their own futures. In the workhouse, officially pauperised and often with little hope of coming out again, the indignities of poverty were heart breaking; Emily Smith, who became a Foleshill Poor Law Guardian in the 1920s, fought to ensure that elderly women inmates were given the pillows and knickers that had until then been deemed unnecessary and withheld.

Gertrude Tuckwell, social campaigner and labour activist, recalled her father, vicar of Stockton in Warwickshire, coming home from an early morning visit to an old woman who always took interest and pleasure in life but lived with the terrible fear that her money would run out before she died. That morning, she had died and the Reverend Tuckwell thanked God for His intervention, thus preventing her from having to enter the workhouse. On another occasion Miss Tuckwell visited the Southam workhouse to see an old friend and was deeply saddened to see that there, very old women who should be resting were being put to work to look after babies and young children.

When, in 1908, the Old Age Pension was introduced by the Liberal government, it was, despite its many limitations, a lifeline to thousands of people. The pension was non-contributory and rather than being claimed through the Poor Law, it was paid as a right to those over the age of 70, helping to keep them in their homes and freer from the constant anxiety of trying to save for the future. It was a small step and one that still made the old

Victorian judgement about the deserving and undeserving poor (it could be refused to those who had been in prison, had recently claimed poor relief or who were judged to be drunks) but it recognised the basic injustice of being punished for running out of money in old age.

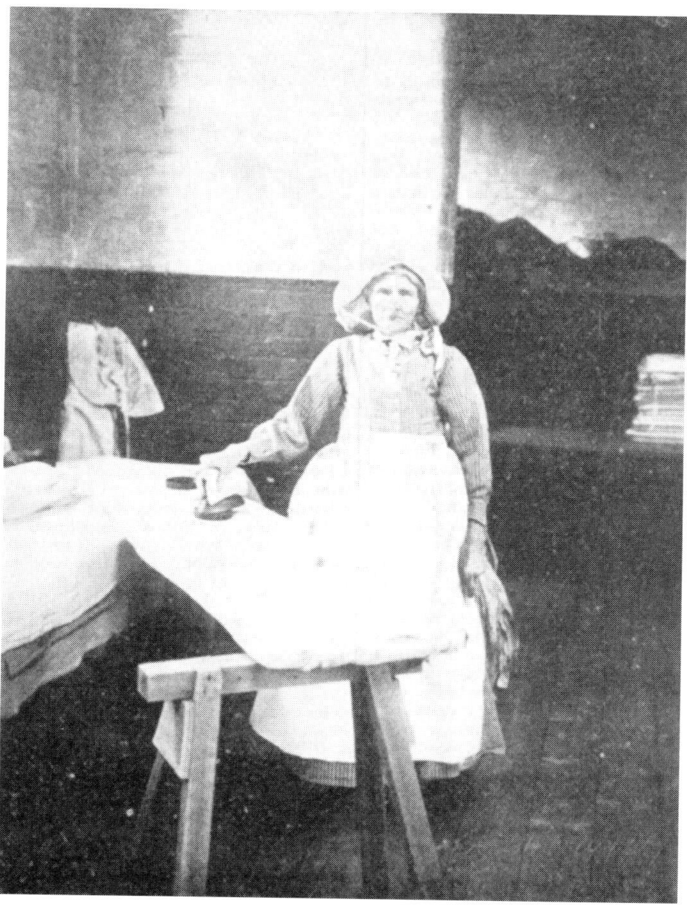

Mrs Sarah Riley, a 97 year old inmate of the Coventry Workhouse. Mrs Riley is seen here working in the laundry, preferring to be busy there than sitting in ease and comfort, according to the *Coventry Graphic* of 25 May 1912. She had, said the Guardians, always lived a respectable life, and now in her extreme old age, refused a whisky night cap but continued to enjoy her daily half pint of beer. *Courtesy of Coventry History Centre*

CHAPTER FIVE

Time to Herself

Like so many women, I have often found it difficult to decide what leisure time actually *is*. There are plenty of things that I like doing that people would instantly recognise as leisure pursuits, such as walking, reading, going to the cinema or to the pub, not to mention taking a holiday. These are no different to what many men also like to do. Sports activities, gardening, art and craft and so on are things we do when we are not working.

A chat over the fence, Coventry women in the early twentieth century. *Courtesy of Albert Smith*

But when we look a little closer, it becomes clearer that much *does* distinguish women's from men's leisure, particularly when we look at the different stages of our lives and what we want to do and – crucially – what time and money we have to be able to do so.

Often, when my family was young, it was all I could do to snatch five minutes to have a cup of tea by myself. Sometimes it was going out for a walk with the pushchair to get the children to sleep while giving myself time to stroll quietly in the park. Just having an uninterrupted bath was an indulgence and a great deal easier for me than many women a hundred years earlier, organising older children to look after younger ones just to allow her a visit to the public slipper baths if time and money allowed, to indulge in instant hot water and the privacy of a booth. Even so, when Priory Street Baths opened in 1894, it was

Priory Street Baths, opened in 1894. *Courtesy of Coventry History Centre*

evident after just a few weeks, that men's attendance at both its swimming and slipper baths was much higher than women's.

Attempts to take breaks, however brief, have been made by mothers throughout the hundred years covered here and have often been more realistic goals than trying to organise a night out when money is tight and babysitters scarce. We might overlook these things because they are unplanned, but, whether we call them leisure, spare time or rest periods, they are undeniably an important part of women's lives.

By looking at how women relaxed, pursued interests and sought entertainment, this chapter reveals a great deal about their hopes and expectations depending on age, income, marital status and family ties. It also highlights gendered differences, from boys who did fewer household chores than their sisters, to men who expected to spend regular time away from the family, in the pub, club, stadium, allotment or river bank, with a portion of their wage unquestioningly put by each week to

Sisters and daughters all set for an outing, around 1910. In the centre is Mabel Hancox with her young daughters, Doris and Winifred and her sister (on the right) Beatrice Palmer. *Courtesy of Albert Smith*

enable them to do so. No matter how hard they worked and how long the working day, for many men a little leisure time was built into the week, accepted as a reward and necessary breather. Many women never knew how much their husbands earned and just accepted what was handed over to them as housekeeping money. Others took more control, one woman remembering that her mother insisted on her father handing over all of his wages because he was such a spendthrift. A woman born in Henry Street in 1911 remembered that her father was happy to stay in the area, despite the rundown housing, because he was comfortable in the local pubs, whereas her mother, who had little recreation and no hobbies, spent time at home making clothes for her daughter. Using 'spare' time constructively in this way became second nature to a great many wives and mothers.

Judgements and Moral Guidance

Pursuits changed over the hundred years, the working week shortened (for some), real wages increased (for some) and paid holidays were introduced, but the importance of having time to oneself remains timeless. Following on from the fight for education and training, the long working hours and the endless struggle to keep the house clean and the family strong and healthy, we might hope that women could spend any free time that they had exactly as they chose. But, just as society had its views on where women should or shouldn't work, what they should or shouldn't learn and on what sort of mothers they should be, there were many people wishing to express opinions about how women should spend the money that they earned and how they should behave when they were out doing so.

Middle class observers worried that working class men and women were not using their time constructively, either for the good of their moral and educational advancement or for the benefit of the wider community. In the 1860s, rail excursions and pedestrian rambles were praised for their superiority over 'the pot-house and the skittle alley'. In fact, every decade seemed to have a fresh moral panic about recreations regarded as unwholesome and when young women were concerned, these generally revolved around being flighty, flirty or behaving too much like men.

In September 1851 the *Coventry Herald and Observer* condemned the 'pernicious' cheap weekly periodicals on sale in Coventry, many of which contained nothing but 'trashy novels'. The paper did not single out girls for criticism; robber and bandit stories were read by 'half-educated' boys and men not accustomed to reading in boyhood, whereas the half-educated girls read the 'silly love tales' and together, the 'neglected lower classes' were forming the worst possible tastes. At a Girls' Friendly Society conference in Rugby in 1889, a paper was delivered about the infinite scope for work to be done among factory girls, whose 'evenings, their Sundays and in many cases the greater part of their Saturdays were their own, and the monotonous life they led caused them to seek recreation in places where it was undesirable for pure-minded girls to go'. What was needed, it was reckoned, was someone with sufficient tact to find out how best to interest these girls and lead them (in the eyes of the concerned) towards a more joyous life. There was widespread concern that factory girls, in their quest to let their hair down after work, were being drawn towards frivolous entertainment and that the impure atmosphere of the music hall or promenading on the streets with their friends would lead them straight into the path of temptation. When Reverend Nye, curate at St Michael's, set out his plans for a 'People's Hall' in 1889, based in a former factory in Earl Street, he made it clear that the aim was for so-called 'rational' amusement, which included making people laugh without putting a wrong idea in their heads. Plans included lectures illustrated with the optical lantern and a 'working girls' Parlour' and Nye's hope was that 'the girls of Coventry, who now have no place but the streets to frolic in, will have many a fine romp in the People's Hall'. In a public appeal for funds in December, he stressed how girls would 'go wrong' without such a place of recreation for sewing, reading, and writing classes as well as running races, swinging to their hearts' content, dancing or having any reasonable fun

A summer picnic for Sunday School teachers of Well Street Methodist Church, 1915. *Courtesy of David Fry*

they liked, so essential after a long day at work. The ultimate aim was then revealed: 'in time, if not at first, they will be ready to seek [religious] instruction'.

During the First World War, the local press noted that girls were no longer content with low starting wages (had they ever been?) and despite their patriotic work and the long shifts demanded, there was concern that they had too much money to know what to do with it. It was said that they did not spend wisely, they bought too many clothes and chocolates, went out too often and got into all sorts of trouble. Early in 1916 an official survey was conducted in Coventry to determine whether there had been an increase in drinking among women since the start of the war. The national Liquor Control Board and the Coventry branch of the Women's Co-operative Guild compiled a list of questions for social workers and nurses to ask in the city and they concluded that drinking had not increased among the wives of soldiers and sailors but that the factory welfare committees were apparently needed to enforce against the strong temptation to smuggle wines and spirits into the workshops, particularly at night.

The presence of so many young women workers living away from home in the city during wartime, out on the streets at night in groups, caused considerable moral panic; the Free Church Girls' Guild stressed the importance of young women forming wise friendships, of preparing them for useful service by means of Reading, Study, Handicrafts, First Aid, Home Nursing, Housewifery and Allotment Cultivation, providing healthy recreation as a means to realising a healthy mind in a healthy body. This was hardly the simple chance to let off a bit of steam that many women munitions workers needed between or after shifts. But for the vast majority, relaxation did not mean a night of drinking; one Irish munitions worker said that it was terrible if you went into a pub and so she kept with her own gang of friends to whom the men were always perfect gentlemen. Their Saturday night entertainment was generally the same – a play at the Hippodrome – while during the week, they made use of the recreation rooms at the hostel.

Family Time

In the nineteenth century, the week-long neighbourhood festivals, known as wakes, were opportunities for family fun, with fairground attractions, shows and sports days as well as dancing and drinking centred on the local pubs. In 1880 swings and 'steam horses' were installed in various parts of Foleshill for its wake, with the Monday and Tuesday observed as general holidays. The South Street School log-book noted 'a wretched attendance' during the Hillfields' festivities in 1894, a combination, perhaps of pupils joining in the fun but also staying up late to mind the younger children while their parents let their hair down. Although employers were under no legal obligation to provide pay for these days off, over time some firms accepted that to do so would be good for morale and in the long run, might even benefit production.

Many women remembered family outings. Mrs Emes, born in Foleshill in 1908, went out with her family in a borrowed pony and trap and picnics in the fields around Blackberry Lane and Miller's Brook. In the inter-war years, Mrs Simmons' family did lots of things together, from singing to listening to the gramophone to walking into the countryside from Stoke and right out to Ryton and Bubbenhall. She didn't recall her parents ever going out and leaving the children but instead there were family visits to the cinema and to the theatre for the pantomime. With the rise in popularity and affordability of the radio, and eight million licences purchased by 1939, an enormous variety of entertainment came to the home. In 1946 a BBC Listener Report surveyed housewives to find out when best to run the programmes that would appeal to them, excluding the late evenings, by far the nation's peak listening time. The results

Coventry railway station, opened in 1838 and rebuilt in 1846 with further changes made during the late nineteenth century. Cheap excursion trains gave families the chance to spend long days out and holidays at seaside resorts and to visit cities and beauty spots. *Courtesy of David Fry*

showed that the hours between eleven and two and four until seven were housewives' most unlikely listening time. All over the country, at these times, women were shopping, collecting children from school, preparing midday meals, feeding babies, getting them down for naps, clearing up and then gearing up to more or less repeat the routine in the afternoon. So, in 1950 the Light Programme schedule included Housewives' Choice at ten past nine in the morning, with Music While You Work at ten forty five. Woman's Hour was at two pm, followed by Music for the Housewife at three.

The coming of the railway allowed those families who could afford it to venture further than the Warwickshire countryside surrounding the city and cheap excursion trains offered day trips and even the possibility of short holidays; in 1884, Gaze's Continental Tours offered a special trip from Coventry to Paris which, with hotel expenses, four-in-hand carriage drives, a conductor's assistance and sundry expenses, cost £4 9*d*. As this was up to four times higher than the wages of many Coventry men and up to eight times higher than the amount earned by many women, this was a treat for those in the professions or those doing well enough to have built up savings beyond an emergency fund. More affordable in good times were day trips to London, to other cities and to seaside resorts including Llandudno, Blackpool and Scarborough. In 1884 the *Coventry Herald* reported that cheap excursions gave hundreds of thousands of people the chance to visit Britain's picturesque spots and romantic natural scenery. Certainly, when all went to plan, such breaks were a breather for all the family (apart from those who had to get up at some ungodly hour to make up picnic hampers for what was often a very long day out) or for groups of friends.

Parents would want reassurances that their daughters travelled safely; the lone female traveller was regarded as vulnerable and at risk of attracting the uninvited and inappropriate attention of men. For those who could afford them there were ladies' only carriages (often first class) but on the 'monster' excursion trains – so long that they had to be pulled by more than one engine – men and women travelled together, in compartments of six to eight which could only be opened onto the platform. In April 1889 a Coventry man was convicted of assaulting passengers in his carriage, including a woman who, after being pushed about and having her cloak torn, managed to get out to ride on the step, jumping off before the train had come to a stop at the station. The man, who was very drunk at the time of the incident, was sentenced to three months in prison for the assaults. It appeared that the communication cord in the carriage was not working, leaving the passengers extremely vulnerable until the station was reached.

Such trains were made use of by firms organising works' trips for employees and their families. In August 1894 two excursions put on by the Coventry silk ribbon firm, J & J Cash, were heavily subscribed; 1,280 people went to Scarborough, leaving Coventry at midnight, arriving in Scarborough at seven in the morning, spending twelve hours at the seaside before getting home to Coventry in the early hours of the following morning. Excursions were not always terribly well organised; an 1866 late summer excursion train returning from Edinburgh was horribly overcrowded with a sole engine that struggled to pull the large number of carriages, causing it to travel at no more than ten miles an hour for sections of the journey. After a twelve-hour journey, passengers for Coventry were set down in a station siding to wait – without refreshments or seating – for a mail train to hopefully convey them onto Birmingham. Things became heated as passengers were left in the dark over whether they were in the right carriages to get home at all. When they finally arrived into Birmingham at three in the morning, the last train to Coventry had left and their ordeal continued until they could board the first scheduled morning train. The whole trip was condemned in the local press as dangerous, a miracle that the passengers, subjected to perils and hazards, escaped with their lives, given the excursion's total disregard for timetabling.

Works outings continued to be patronised well into the twentieth century and as an Act of Parliament in 1938 extended the right to paid holiday from three to over eleven million people,

Beatrice Callow, author of Hurdy Gurdy Days, at a holiday chalet in Rhyl in 1930. *Courtesy of Anne Callow*

the chance of a week away, making use of cheap transport or even – for the better off – the family car – became a reality. By the 1930s Coventry factories were closing for a week in August and the Coventry and District Co-operative Society was running advertisements for its 'Coventry by the Sea' holiday camp near Rhyl. This was before the advent of Butlins and facilities were basic, to say the least; for 1932 there were promises of improved sanitary arrangements and lavatory conveniences for both sexes. Ten bell tents for families were being replaced with ten large huts, alongside smaller huts, square tents and space for those who wished to pitch their own tents. Rhyl had plenty of competition for its 'Coventry by the sea' tag line; in June 1939, ahead of what the *Midland Daily Telegraph* called a Coventry invasion, the mayor of Ramsgate urged the town's landladies to make Coventry folk feel at home and to make sure that they had the finest holiday of their lives.

A Coventry charabanc outing, early 20th century. *Courtesy of David Fry*

Middle-class Women

The nineteenth century ideal was, as we have seen, for a man to earn enough to support his family and place his wife at the domestic heart of his home, her appearance and demeanour reflecting his status in the community. Among the middle classes, a wife might aim to give the illusion of being a woman at leisure, priding herself on running an efficient, organised household. In reality, how much time she spent ordering food, planning meals, clothing her children, decorating her house, arranging her husband's comforts and managing the daily budget, depended entirely on how many servants she had, how trusted they were and on how much she was allowed or able to do, in between giving birth and nurturing children.

The distinctions between social duty, etiquette and leisure were often blurred; the leisured woman was expected to make a fulltime job of being amenable, available and busy at the same time. The accomplishments learnt in youth ensured that her hands were never idle. Decorative sewing, such as sampler embroidering, sketching and piano playing were all activities with which to while away time and to show off the outcome of a useful education. But, as Florence Nightingale wrote in *Cassandra* in 1852, women had to expect interruption, pursuits were to be put down or picked up to suit those she was in company with, and there was no time to call her own. She was not supposed to study any subject deeply but instead learn just enough to allow her to engage in polite – but never intellectual – conversation. In addition there were calling cards to leave, guests to receive, dinner parties to arrange and attend and, depending on income, status and local standing, charitable and church events to attend or to organise. Such activities might be gratefully sought as worthy employment by the restless, bored middle-class woman or resented as the necessary, expected work of the monied classes.

Then again, there were opportunities to combine pleasure with duty, possibly seized on by young women who had more time and money than their working class sisters, but fewer opportunities to escape the confines of the home. The attendance for the 1893 ball to raise money for the Coventry and Warwickshire Hospital reads like a list of the city's great and good, including the wives and daughters of industrialists and professional men, many of whom were heavily involved in fundraising and organising within a range of good causes such as the Girls' Industrial School, the lying-in charities or the Coventry Philanthropic Society. Sometimes such events might even be fun; in June 1893 the Coventry lady cyclist team accepted an invitation from mayoress Mrs Singer to ride out to her impressive home – Coundon Court – where the women were greeted by the Singers, served tea in the hall, given a tour of the gardens and tennis lawn, treated to a musical entertainment and light refreshments before leaving, led by their captain with Miss Starley bringing up the rear. This was undoubtedly a splendid way to spend a June afternoon for the cyclists and, given that the following year was noted for its large increase in lady cycling, with manufacturers having a 'good deal to thank the ladies for

Ladies' cycling club, Holyhead Road, at the turn of the century. *Courtesy of Coventry History Centre*

in increasing the popularity of the sport', useful publicity for both the Singer and Starley cycle businesses.

The Open Road

In fact, for those women who could afford it, the bicycle offered freedom, exhilaration and an escape from the sedate ladylike pursuits they were supposed to favour. As bicycles changed from the cumbersome models that appealed to daring, sporting young men, to those easier to use, they became increasingly popular not just for sport and leisure, but as practical modes of transport. The *Coventry Herald* was confident that by 1893 the lady cyclist no longer caused a sensation as she passed along the street. The public, it declared, had become reconciled to this innovation, although it still seemed necessary to offer reassurance that cycling could be undertaken with decorum, with women presenting a thoroughly dignified appearance as they rode along. The important mastering of dignity was, the paper thought, partly due to women's efforts to master the bicycle on secluded lanes with no risk of recognition as they displayed remarkable zeal and energy, appearing in public only when they could attain grace and agility. What to wear was also a matter of concern; it was not easy to ride wearing a long skirt that could tangle into the back wheel of the cycle but there was widespread disapproval of those women who favoured the trend for so-called 'rational dress', which included knickerbockers or breeches and rather masculine tailored jackets. By 1893 the *Coventry Herald* seemed relieved that lady cyclists in England were mostly retaining their traditional skirts, unlike their French counterparts who were said to be flouting French law by dressing in men's clothes – namely the tunics and short breeches of the men's cycling clubs. The idea behind rational dress was partly to encourage less restrictive and healthier forms of clothing but there was deep suspicion of those for whom dress reform was just one aspect of a move towards emancipation for women.

Women cyclists at Coombe Fields, 1912. *Courtesy of David Fry*

The 'New Woman' of the 1890s, mocked for her unladylike appearance and manners, was unfavourably compared in the *Coventry Herald* with the Princess of Wales who, at 50 in 1894, was 'all sweetness and grace', glorying in her wifehood and motherhood and 'not only her husband and children but the people rise up and call her blessed'. In the provinces, only the brave would risk being seen in public in knickerbockers and it was more common for women cyclists either to try a divided skirt or to look for ways to adapt their usual clothes.

The bicycle became even more popular as it became cheaper and working-class women who could afford to buy either a new or second-hand machine were able to journey into the countryside, literally expanding their horizons by travelling independently – or at least without parents or chaperones. A number of cycling clubs were formed in Coventry, giving opportunities to some

Muriel Hind, competitive motorcycle rider, 1910. *Courtesy of the Herbert Art Gallery & Museum, Coventry*

superb sportswomen, including Edith Atkins, who got her first bicycle in 1933 when she was 13. Three years later, she was one of the founder members of the Coventry Meteor Cycling Club and went on to excel in track and road events, in 1953 beating the professional record for the Lands End to John O' Groats race.

Just as it was for Edith Atkins, Muriel Hind's life was irrevocably changed by the cycle; in 1902, aged 21, she bought her first motorcycle made by Singer and three years later, entered her first competition, the only female entrant. Over the next few years, she won, among other awards, five gold medals in London to Edinburgh runs. Writing for motorcycle newspapers, manufacturers began to ask Hind to test and review new models for them and in 1907, Coventry's Rex Motor Manufacturing Company produced its 'Blue Devil' machine, to her specification. Always mindful of her extraordinary participation in an almost exclusively male sport, Hind felt the need to dress with care; her distinctive style included a hat fixed on securely with a scarf, a long thick coat and knee length boots. In 1931 she became the first woman life member of the Association of Pioneer Motor Cyclists.

The Sporting Life

Once adaptations to the bicycle had removed the objections of the prudish, cycling came to be regarded as a healthy, useful and dignified pursuit for women. Its popularity encouraged the acceptance of women's participation in a wider range of sports than previously, amid a growing understanding of the benefits of physical exercise, although much caution was still urged. In 1894 Mrs Dr Potts, of the Women's Medical College of Philadelphia, gave a lecture on women's health at the Opera House on Hales Street. She warned her audience of the 'evil consequences of violent and long sustained exertion' in such exercises as skipping, riding, rowing, skating and athletics.

Although many city schools had little or no room to provide field sports, pupils were encouraged to use the new city swimming

Factory sports clubs were an important part of many women's lives.
Courtesy of the Herbert Art Gallery & Museum, Coventry

baths and in 1896 Kate Cowley, a pupil at Wheatley Street Girls School, won the championship and silver medal offered by the Council for the fastest girl swimmer in its elementary schools. Swedish drill – a form of gymnastics – grew in popularity at the turn of the century and was advertised as part of the curriculum at the Quadrant private girls' school in 1894. When Barr's Hill School opened, its extensive grounds ensured that there was space for tennis, drill and, with the loan of a neighbour's field in 1914, it was hoped to offer cricket as well.

The Coventry branch of the all-female trade union, the National Federation of Women Workers, set up a cricket team in 1908 and by the First World War there were several different ladies' cricket teams raising money for the war effort. When women competed against men, it was regarded as sporting to insist that the men bat left-handed and bowl underarm. With this in mind, the report of a match between the Magneto Ladies Cricket and a team of soldiers and sailors in 1918 was, then, rather unnecessarily grudging, commenting that the imposed handicaps proved too much for the men, leading the ladies to an easy victory!

Hotchkiss and Cie Factory sports' event at the Butts Stadium, in the summer of 1917. *Courtesy of David Fry*

Women's football also became very popular during the First World War, with many munitions factories building teams and playing to very large crowds. By this time, the warnings carried in the *Coventry Herald* in 1894 by the *British Medical Journal* appear to have subsided, presumably lost amid a growing realisation that women were capable of withstanding much tougher challenges than a game of football. Back then it had stated that while it was harmless enough for girls to kick a ball around between lessons, a proper game was another matter, exposing girls to the 'reckless exposure to violence of organs which the common experience of women has led them in every way to protect'. The chances of injury were too high unless, stated the writer, they were prepared to advocate artificial infant feeding and ignore the proper use of the breast. While these concerns might have been put aside by 1917, journalists were still sometimes rather incredulous that women knew what to do on the pitch, with the *Midland Daily Telegraph* reporting after a September tournament at the Butts in aid of French Flag Day

Team from ladies' football tournament organised by Rudge-Whitworth at the Butts Stadium in March 1917. *Courtesy of David Fry*

Girls' swimming club at Courtaulds' open air pool at the works. *Coventry Graphic,* 22 June 1912. *Courtesy of Coventry History Centre*

that the ladies had played very well, with several of them having an excellent idea of the game. After the war, as so many sections of society sought to restore the country to more traditional ways of life, the Football Association refused women's teams the use of its pitches from 1921. Many women retained a love of competitive sport that they had not encountered in elementary schools but the progress of organised women's football was indisputably put back many years by this ban.

By the Second World War, Coventry had women's teams and clubs playing a range of sports, including golf, netball and hockey. One way of becoming involved was at work, with many factories promoting participation in sports, including tapping into the inter-war craze for keep fit. The Women's League of

A Coventry League of Health and Beauty class in the 1930s. *Courtesy of the Herbert Art Gallery & Museum, Coventry*

Health and Beauty, with its motto of 'Movement is Life' was formed in 1930 and in 1937 Courtaulds' house magazine, *The Rayoneer*, informed its women readers that the League now had fifty centres across the country and 90,000 women members. Reminding them that it was never too late or too early to learn, it explained the League's emphasis on retaining femininity ('no over developed muscles and unattractive athleticism') and promised that a course of the rhythmic, joint-loosening exercises would appear next month. In November 1939 the League was urging Coventry members to 'Keep Fit and Forget your Worries' and in 1944, the President of Coventry's Keep Fit Classes, the author Angela Brazil, congratulated the members on how fit they looked after five years of war. It was a release of sorts.

Dancing the Night Away (sometimes as late as 10.45pm…)

The synchronised routines performed to music might have appealed to those women who loved to dance and from the dancing parties in pubs during wakes' weeks in the nineteenth century, to the more formal balls attended by middle-class men and women, many young women relished every opportunity to let off steam and show off their talents on the dance floor. By the 1920s dancing had become a national craze. The First World War had provided lots of opportunities to dance, with factories, trade unions and girls' clubs all competing for women workers' attendance at their organised events. An official report on welfare conditions among Coventry's war workers in 1916 concluded that there was too little organised provision for recreation in the city, with 'Picture Palaces and walking the dark streets' the only alternatives for those in hostels and lodgings. What was needed was 'a bright central meeting-place' for 'wholesome amusement' including dancing, music and games as well as for quieter pursuits. As well as keeping women off those dark streets and away from the cinemas, dances were also a way of raising money for wartime causes and for burning off nervous energy after long, monotonous shifts on the factory floor.

The promise of dancing was an effective way of bringing women together to hear about the benefits of trade union membership. According to the National Federation of Women Workers, a 'jolly set of girls' turned out on a wet winter's evening to the Co-operative Assembly Rooms in West Orchard in 1916 and dancing was in full swing by seven thirty. During the interval, the Union's national organising secretary, Margaret Bondfield, addressed the girls and then dancing continued until ten forty five 'with a very strong desire among the girls that a similar social should take place weekly'. This left just enough time to get back to the hostels, as long as a late pass (up to eleven thirty) had been given. A spring dance organised by the mixed-sex Workers' Union was a success despite the fact that 'owing to a large number of the "best boys" being at the Front, the pretty sex predominated'. The women's organiser, Julia Varley, determined to be positive, reported that 'owing to the sombre attire of mere men, the effect was very dainty, most of the girls being in light colours'. Even the Young Women's Christian Association Club, opened in Park Road in 1917 for munitions workers, advocated the importance of dancing in helping young women appreciate the value of 'true fun and amusement', at the same time protecting them from the 'dangers that followed on the social disintegration of these times and [making] them fit and helpful citizens of the future England'.

Many of those citizens went on to have a great deal of true fun and amusement after the war, at ballrooms such as the Gaumont on Jordan Well and the Rialto on Moseley Avenue, and also in those built by the city's manufacturing firms, with the largest and most prestigious belonging to the GEC and nicknamed 'The Conner'. In 1925 the GEC's *Loudspeaker* magazine boasted that the firm had the best dance floor in Coventry, an orchestra that was 'all that can be desired' and as a result, the popularity of Saturday night dances was increasing every year. Dancing, it reckoned, was a natural and harmless outlet for young men and women with vigorous health and rampant spirits, as long as, it warned, it was 'the right kind' of dancing and it was down to the older folks to see 'that the

The Magnet Club Ballroom at the GEC, often called 'The Conner', reckoned by the firm to be the best dance floor in Coventry. *The Loudspeaker,* January 1929. *Courtesy of Coventry History Centre*

freedom of the modern girl is not allowed to develop into licence'!

During the Second World War, dance events helped to raise money for the war effort. In May 1943 the Hippodrome held a Wings for Victory gala, with a personal appearance by Charles Shadwell, the BBC's Variety conductor leading the Hippodrome Broadcasting Orchestra, the Massed Bands of the RAF and the WAAF and radio stars, including Jack Warner and Mrs Mop of ITMA. As part of its 'grand Stay-At-Home Holiday Dance Programme' in 1943, the Rialto Casino offered tea dances, a crazy costume dance and a 'come in your glad rags and hang the coupons' dance. The newspapers were full of advertisements for dances; in 1942 young men were urged to come along to the Savoy Ballroom where they would be sure to meet that girl during non-stop dancing between seven and ten. Open-air dances were also popular; in August 1942, the Coventry On Holiday events included bands and dancing in the Memorial Park. When Brooklands Hostel in Coundon opened in 1942 for workers on government production, it included recreational rooms and a dance hall with dancing nearly every night. According to the welfare officer, discipline was not strict and all that was needed was common sense; men were allowed out until any time but girls were expected to be in their sleeping quarters within a quarter of an hour of any arranged entertainment finishing!

Footloose and Fancy Free

Just how much leisure time young single working-class women achieved depended on the nature of their work and on how much – or little – money they had to spend on themselves. Not all female workers benefited from gradually shortening working weeks and often, the less they earned, the longer the hours worked. In many of the jobs associated with women, time off was extremely hard to come by; employers did not always respect the right of domestic servants to have time to themselves, the working day of an Edwardian shop assistant could be up to fifteen hours long, with shops not shutting until eleven at night.

Nonetheless, the years between leaving school and getting married were those in which young women were likely to have the most time to themselves, despite numerous constraints, including money. In 1928 Mrs Bucknell, then aged 14, left school to work in an elastic making factory. She gave ten of her eleven and a half shillings wage to her mother and with the remaining money paid her own chapel collection, Girl Guides subs and visits to the cinema with sweets. Money was still handed over to parents as girls got older and there was little spare cash to spend on having fun. Going to 'early doors' at the cinema was one way of saving a bit of money, with Mrs Purnell remembering that in the early 1920s, if Mr Jordan was on the door at the old Hippodrome, near Pool Meadow, he might even let her and her friends in for nothing at half time. In the inter-war years, cinema became enormously popular; it was cheap and it was an acceptable place for a young woman to go with friends.

The Hippodrome Theatre, Hales Street. This is the second of three theatres on or near this site, this one opening in 1906. *Courtesy of David Fry*

Although the cinema features heavily in accounts of inter-war life – unsurprising, given that Coventry had over twenty cinemas by 1939 – for some girls it caused conflict with other parts of their lives; one woman recalled the guilt she felt about going to the pictures on a Sunday after church – but she went anyway.

Mrs Dingley was born in Coventry in 1900 and her memories of free time start with an account of leaving work at Fred Lee's jewel works early on Saturday afternoons and heading into town to Woolworth's on Smithford Street. Here there was a piano on a platform, the girls would select some sheet music and ask the pianist to play it for them to decide if, for sixpence, they wanted to buy it. The idea was that they could then learn the tune from those girls who knew how to play. After an hour or so at Woolworth's, they might go to a musical comedy at the Old Opera House in Hales Street, though at a shilling a ticket, this was quite an expense. When this finished, at five thirty, they would all rush home to get ready to go back out to the Empire,

The Empire Cinema, Hertford Street. Originally the Corn Exchange in 1856, it became the Empire Theatre in 1907, showing films throughout the 1920s. It re-opened after a fire in 1931 but was once again damaged during the Second World War. *Courtesy of Coventry History Centre*

at the top of Hertford Street, where the first dance (for two and a half pence) started at six thirty. When they came out, they might head down to Market Street and just all walk around for a few hours before going to the Hippodrome on Hales Street for the second showing (four pence). That, she said, took care of your week's pocket money and if you wanted to go to the Empire on Sunday night, you would have to borrow money for a ticket (another four pence). It was cheaper to go to Naul's Mill Park on Sunday afternoon to listen to the band – three pence if you wanted a deckchair, but free to just wander around.

Another form of free amusement was that known locally as the Bunny Run, where young men and women in their glad rags would stroll with their friends and size each other up, just for fun or in search of the promise of a date. Before her marriage, Mrs Purnell used to go with a friend; the Run started on New Union Street, continued along Warwick Road and up onto the Kenilworth Road. It was important to stay close to friends – May's friend would beg her not to leave her or even stray from her side.

Stylised athleticism in early 20th century Coventry. *Courtesy of David Fry*

Belonging

As well as nights out and nights in, there were women whose social life and free time revolved around their membership of, or involvement in, one or more organisations. Their varied interests and talents led them to orchestral societies, choirs and amateur dramatics, to cycling and rambling clubs and to more sedate activities, including writing and painting. Many, as we have seen, attended evening classes, sometimes for pleasure, sometimes to advance their careers. Others, as we will see in the final chapter, devoted all the time they had to working for the greater good of the community, engaging in political or philanthropic roles. All of these roles serve to remind us that women, like men, have a great range of interests. When Courtaulds' magazine asked its women readers in 1937, what was their pet recreation, it answered the question for them; knitting, it supposed, headed the list. I wouldn't be so sure.

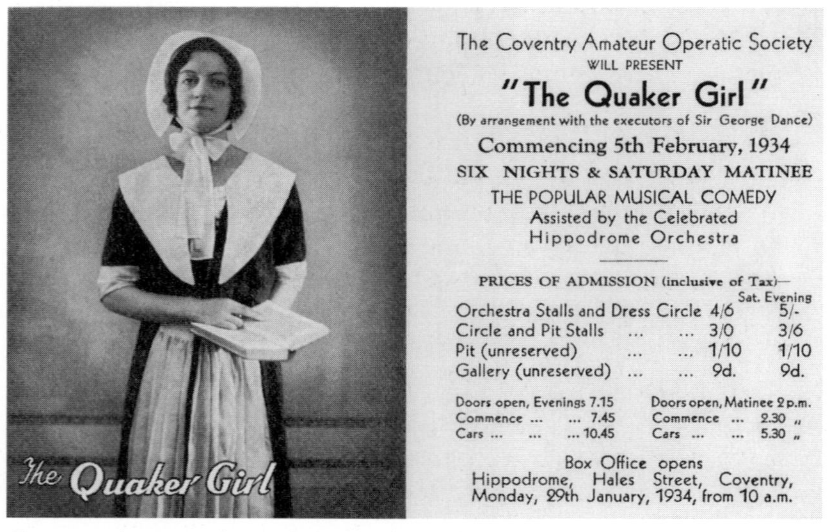

Coventry Amateur Operatic Society's production of *The Quaker Girl,* 1934. *Courtesy of David Fry*

CHAPTER SIX

For the Common Good

In 1945 Coventry City Council prepared to celebrate the 600th anniversary of its charter of incorporation. Speaking in support of a permanent memorial to mark the event, Alice Arnold, longstanding councillor and alderman, and Coventry's first woman mayor in 1937, said that this would speak not only for the men but for the women who had served Coventry through the ages. She began with Lady Godiva, adding that although people often joke about her,

> Whatever may be said, it is the fact that from the very dawn of time this city's history comes the memory of a woman, and a very beautiful woman at that, who made a sacrifice to help those who could not help themselves. That is the central meaning of the old story and it is a fine and inspiring one.

Alderman Arnold went on to pay tribute to other women who had served the city, including Queen Isabella, who granted the Charter. She was a woman who 'knew her own mind' and who had taken an immense interest in the city and who could, when necessary, put the Prior and the Bailiffs in their place'. Then, said the alderman, there were the Botoner sisters, Anne and Mary, who built the lovely spire of St Michael's Church and Mary Herbert, who, during the Civil War, with the city expecting an attack from the Royalist army, 'led forth the women of Coventry to dig trenches in the Park … an officer of

Godiva Procession, with Maude Forester in the leading role, 1883. *Courtesy of David Fry*

the [Auxiliary Territorial Service] before her time'. There were charities begun by Elizabeth Swillington and Catherine Bayley which still benefited Coventry people. Lastly, she remembered George Eliot and her schooldays in the city. Many women could be mentioned, said the alderman but she felt that was not necessary because;

> I can say … on behalf of the women of Coventry, that they desire to serve their city to the utmost of their power, side by side with the men. The great interest which the women of today take in city affairs – shown not only by their seeking membership of public bodies, but in many other ways – is very appropriate in a city which has owed so much to women. I expect that if some of the women of the past whom I have mentioned were today able to

> be present in this hall, which many of them knew so well, they would be surprised to see a woman alderman on this platform taking part in a meeting of the City Council, but I think they would approve it.

She added that she and her female colleagues were building on a foundation laid for them by those women of the past and she was certain that in another hundred years' time, citizens would be proud to know that at the 600th anniversary of their city, a place was given to a woman speaker.

These powerful words form the perfect introduction for a chapter that looks at the ways in which, as well as working hard, raising families, making ends meet, breaking through barriers in all aspects of life, women also endeavoured to campaign and work for change and reform on behalf of others, at both the national and local level. They also serve as a reminder that women's involvement in public life, despite many suggestions to the contrary, did not start with the fight for the vote. The Edwardian campaign for women's votes attracted an enormous amount of attention; the tactics used were daring and they divided public

Alice Arnold, Labour Councillor, Alderman and first woman Mayor of Coventry, 1937.
Courtesy of Coventry History Centre

Selina Dix (1859-1942). Born in Beeston, Nottinghamshire, she became head teacher of South Street School in 1889 and of Wheatley Street School in 1893. Miss Dix worked with a range of local government and campaigning organisations with an emphasis on improving the lives of women and children. *Coventry Graphic*, 16 December 1911. *Courtesy of Coventry History Centre*

opinion. The outspokenness of its activists challenged the old Victorian view that women had no place in the public world and should be shielded from politics and protected from its complications by husbands and fathers.

Selina Dix, headmistress of Wheatley Street Girls' School and President of the Warwickshire County Association of the National Union of Teachers (NUT), gently challenged this view at the Association's Annual Meeting of 1914. As Alice Arnold was later to do, she referred to women throughout time who had acquired fame and who had been strong enough to make their power felt for good or ill. Yet, she asked how women as a whole were regarded, quoting George Lyttleton's 1731 poem, 'Advice to a Lady'; 'Seek to be good, but aim not to be great, a noblest woman's station is retreat', as well as an early Alfred Tennyson poem declaring that 'Woman is the lesser man'. But, she said, 'women now demand – and are often considered unreasonable in doing so – … that work which is open to men should not be closed to women' who had proved their talents and capabilities in leadership, science, art, literature, mathematics and medicine. Calling for professional equality and pay, Miss Dix was sure that, '[a] Woman in the place that will be afforded her will express her own individuality, she will possess the right to serve, the right to reform, the right to still the pain of the world.'

'Stilling the pain'

In the nineteenth century, Coventry women who could afford to do so, sought ways to 'still that pain' from within their accepted roles as carers and nurturers. They did not always understand the realities of the lives of those they sought to help and as a result their interventions could sometimes be patronising and unwelcome but they regarded it as their Christian duty to help the respectable, deserving poor. When the ribbon industry crashed with devastating consequences in 1860, relief funds were set up, soup kitchens established and a committee of women set about collecting and distributing clothes to families in need. The following winter a needlework society was formed by 'some benevolent ladies' of the city, offering work to 'respectable women' as a means of supporting themselves at this time of high unemployment. In October 1862, the *Coventry Times* carried a rather surprising commentary on the young women clustered about the doors of the city's ribbon manufacturing establishments. Clothed in 'tattered, thin calico dresses, and wrapped in shawls which would, in more prosperous times have not for a moment been tolerated in daylight, we recognise those who a few years back were well-clad members of society'. The paper speculated that given the meanness of the outside show, 'what must be said of their undergarments?' These, it was suggested, were in such a state as to cause shame and confusion to their poverty-stricken owners if they were not concealed. Instead of parting with their 'rags', simply because the initial gloss had worn off, ladies could give these to charity, rather than to the ragman, and help to keep poor women warm in inclement weather. This clothing question, it was felt, fell 'peculiarly within the women's province, and, if they go heartily into it we are sure it may be satisfactorily solved'.

Visiting the poor was another accepted role for Victorian women. When the Ladies' Visiting Committee was established at the Coventry Workhouse in 1890, the efforts of the appointed women were not always met with gratitude either by the elected Poor Law Guardians or by the workhouse Master. Originally three women from the Church of England and three from the non-conformist churches were appointed to visit workhouse schoolchildren. By 1893 the committee had grown to fifteen and there were some concerns from the (male) Guardians that some of these women were overstepping the mark and 'meddling' in affairs that they had no business in, sending servants or nurses to fetch keys so that they could inspect food items, for example. One lady visitor had discovered that the workhouse milk had been sour two days running but instead of bringing this to the attention of the Master or the Matron, as the Guardians did, she complained directly to a Guardian. At a Guardians' meeting, it was alleged that 'the ladies are not so courteous to the Master as the Guardians are' and that if they

Coventry Poor Law Guardians in 1913. In the dark hat is Mrs Keene, representing Swanswell Ward and in the light hat is Mrs Griffiths, for All Saints' Ward. The hatless woman may be the Workhouse Matron (E Martin). *Courtesy of Coventry History Centre*

went about their work 'in a nice, quiet, unofficious manner no one would find fault with them'. One very disgruntled male Guardian stated that 'if the ladies stayed at home and looked after their own domestic affairs and left us to do the business of the Board we should all get on all right'. It is difficult to assess what was actually going on here, whether the lady visitors regarded themselves as being above the established proceedings of the workhouse or whether the elected Poor Law officials objected to them voicing concerns about the safety and wellbeing of the inmates and thereby implicitly criticising the work that they had been doing.

Poor Law Guardians and Public Service

Although in theory women could become Poor Law Guardians from 1832, it was not until 1875 that the first woman was elected as a Guardian in London. In other parts of the country, numbers remained small until the 1894 Local Government Act altered the property qualifications, making it easier for women to stand for election. Even so, there were undoubtedly some men who were unhappy about the advent of women Guardians, claiming that they would have to deal with unseemly matters in the workhouse. On the contrary, women made it clear that this was a role that they were entirely suited to. Among the first women elected in Coventry were Amy Hurlston and Mrs M. Haywood. At their first meeting in January 1895, Miss Hurlston thanked the Board for the welcome given to her and Mrs Haywood and said that she was glad to be associated with gentlemen in the management of so important an institution as the workhouse. She went a little further; it was more than she expected because in public affairs, women were generally looked upon as being little better than fools. But, she continued, as George Eliot wrote, 'God made some foolish women to match the men'. Some of the men were amused by her remarks, the majority were not and hisses were heard. This was undoubtedly a bold start for Coventry's first female Guardian who was at the time of her election, only 29.

In 1895 both of these women were assigned to the School Attendance Committee and the Stores Committee, quite possibly because it was felt that they could draw on their supposed feminine strengths and interests – the welfare of children and the domestic running of a household. While women recognised that the Guardians' role was entirely suited to them, the elected men began to realise that there was a great deal that they could leave to the women, including the care of unmarried mothers and babies. When Mrs Haywood stepped down in 1901, after six years, she said that,

> There is more work for a woman to do on the Board of Guardians than there is for a man. She is often called upon to do more behind the scenes, as it were, and it leads to so many other things … what with committee meetings, visiting, investigating cases, writing notes and the thousand and one applications that one receives through being a Guardian, fully a day is absorbed.

Because of the poor health of one of her children, she felt she could no longer continue but was adamant that women's presence on the Board was a necessity, ensuring that delicate cases were dealt with, but warning women that plenty of time was needed to devote to the work.

Not all women who sought election approved of the Poor Law system and in the early twentieth century, several Labour candidates made their feelings plain. Standing for election in 1913, Henrietta Givens said that it was not enough merely to relieve destitution and that she would support any legislation that replaced the Poor Law with a better system. In the meantime (until its abolition in 1929) several Labour women were elected and did their best to make conditions within the workhouse more comfortable and humane. Sarah Griffiths, a Guardian before the First World War, was regularly presented with problems when she was out and about on the streets and would always stop and try to help those in need. Born in 1871, her childhood was spent in some of the poorest parts of the city, including Cook Street, the Chauntries and St John's Street. She was working part time by the time she was 7. She once told a reporter that having to work when she was so young probably helped her to understand other people's problems, adding however, 'I don't like talking about it now – it's all in the past'. Her public career was impressive; she was one of Coventry's first woman magistrates – if women having domestic problems with their husbands came to see her for help, she used to tell them to make sure that the summons was issued on a Tuesday because that was her day on the bench. She received an OBE for First World War work on the local Pensions Committee and as a Guardian. In 1929 when the Poor Law Board was abolished, she was elected a Labour councillor, becoming chair of the Public Assistance Committee and ten years later, an alderman, as an acknowledged senior member of the council.

Coventry's First Women Councillors

It is something of an understatement to say that the advent of women councillors was a significant event – it was momentous. For nearly 600 years, Coventry had been governed entirely by men who in turn had been elected by men (although from 1869 single women ratepayers had the right to vote in local elections). The first to be elected to the Council were Alice Arnold and Ellen Hughes in 1919, in the first municipal elections held after the First World War. By 1939, eleven women had served, all representing Labour, which took control of the City Council for the first time in 1937. The work of these women pioneers made a significant impact on the life of Coventry citizens. Working to represent all their constituents, they drew on expertise from both their political and personal backgrounds to push for practical change. They sought improvements for families, including decent housing, spaces for children to play, nursery schools and expanded maternity and child welfare facilities.

But we should not think for a moment that these women served only from within the caring female roles that society had for so long expected of them. They took their places on a range

The Labour Group on Coventry City Council, 1919. Miss Alice Arnold (left) and Mrs Ellen Hughes were Coventry's first women councillors. *Coventry Graphic*, 14 November 1919. *Courtesy of Coventry History Centre*

of Council committees and celebrated breakthroughs when they came – first committee chairwomen, aldermen and mayors. Some years ago, former Labour MP Bill Wilson told me that he could remember the Labour women councillors far more than he could the men, possibly because of the extra work that they had to put in to be accepted and elected, but also because of the strength of their characters. When Alderman Ellen Hughes died in 1939, she was described as a fighter for great causes. She was, said the Reverend Lee at her funeral, more than an idealist but someone who lived to get things done by her pluck, pertinacity and labour. Alice Arnold, Coventry born and bred, was well known for her personal representation of people in need, accompanying them to court to challenge eviction orders, ensuring that the unemployed in her ward were supported and fed. In doing so, her outspokenness delighted a press not yet used to the idea of women councillors, let alone one who entered politics with such apparent fearlessness. An early example of her forthright style came in 1920 when Prince Albert, the future King George VI officially opened the Council House. Ahead of the visit, she asked whether, after admiring the grandeur of the new building, he might 'see the other side of the picture and visit the filthy slums of the city'. The mayor simply informed her that this would *not* be part of the programme.

Emily Smith, Poor Law Guardian, Labour Councillor, alderman, magistrate and Coventry's second woman mayor, 1942. Coventry Municipal Yearbooks. *Courtesy of Coventry History Centre*

Coventry's two first women mayors – Alice Arnold in 1937 and Emily Smith in 1942 – made a deep impression on the city but both were humbled by their reception wherever they went. Alice Arnold was clearly moved by finding 'so many people trying to do good in their own way' and Emily Smith, facing the challenge of being a wartime mayor, remarked that 'for it to be possible for a working woman to become mayor of this ancient city … speaks highly for our democracy'. Emily Smith came to Coventry from Bradford in 1915 and was widowed four years later. She brought up her children alone and also her granddaughter, after the death of her daughter-in-law. The *Midland Daily Telegraph* praised the mayor's industriousness, noting that she even found time to do her own shopping, leaving

Mrs Henrietta Givens, organiser for the Coventry branch of the National Federation of Women Workers, Coventry's first woman magistrate, 1920 and Labour Councillor 1935-49. Member of the Co-operative Women's Guild. *Coventry Graphic*, 15 March 1913. *Courtesy of Coventry History Centre*

her bag and ration books at the shop and collecting her order when it was made up for her. As she came to the end of a challenging mayoral year, she concluded that 'All I wanted to be [was] a good mother to the citizens'.

The women councillors did not all cut their political teeth on the Poor Law. Both Alice Arnold and Henrietta Givens, elected in 1935, had been trade union organisers during the First World War. Arnold, for the mixed-sex Workers' Union and Givens, for the all-female National Federation of Women Workers, helped to form substantial branches of women workers, most of whom were engaged on munitions' production. They took on employers who were reluctant to pay women the correct rate for the job, they recruited new members, often at the factory gates, and addressed crowds and meetings at short notice. All of this took a strength of character not possessed by all and their efforts to protect women's position in the workplace and promote equality did not go unnoticed by those they sought to help. Alice Arnold was remembered by an Ordnance worker as a wonderful person for working women. Mrs Givens, often working with her trade unionist husband, represented and won cases for women at tribunals and the couple were described by her union as 'our indefatigable friends'.

Women's Co-operative Guild

The majority of those women who served as city councillors in the inter-war years were also members of the Women's Co-operative Guild. Founded in 1883 with the aim 'to educate women in Co-operative principles, and increase their power and activity in the movement', Coventry had one of the country's earliest branches, with its first meeting held in November 1884 under the presidency of Miss Shufflebotham. While campaigning for social change, particularly in relation to women and children, one of the most important aspects of membership was the emphasis placed on helping women to gain the confidence to speak in public. That this could be done in women only meetings of the Guild made a big difference to those who either lacked the courage or never had the chance to speak at Co-operative Society or political meetings where men predominated. Meetings allowed women to learn about new subjects and to debate subjects with other women, safe in the knowledge that their expressed opinions were welcomed and not

The Committee of the Coventry Women's Co-operative Guild, 1917. *Coventry Co-operative Society Jubilee History* 1867-1917. *Courtesy of Coventry History Centre*

drowned out by men. Social functions were also important, one of the first taking place at Miss Shufflebotham's house, Canley Cottage in Whor Lane (now Beechwood Avenue), an alfresco affair for members to enjoy her gardens but also to learn about the behaviour of bees!

Mrs Rea, born in Foleshill, recalled a great deal of loyalty to the Co-operative movement in her area and when she was married she became a member of the Guild. Her personal description of its objective was that it wanted to bring women out of the kitchen and to give them some independence from men. The women who joined, said Mrs Rea, were 'marvellous', inviting speakers (when someone came to talk about birth control, 'the men went frantic') and 'we would take everything to pieces' at meetings.

In the years before and after the First World War, their most effective campaigning was for improved and extended maternity and child welfare. Guild members were well represented on the

The Co-operative Society, reminding Coventry of its continued commitment to maternity and child welfare at Coventry's Labour Day, 1920. The Co-op also offered health insurance, which is being advertised here. *Courtesy of David Fry*

Care of Maternity Committee and, after 1918, on the City Council's Maternity Committee, established by the Maternity and Child Welfare Act of that year. Guild volunteers then played a crucial role in the running of baby clinics as these were established in parts of the city, the City Council providing a doctor and health visitor but the volunteers weighing babies, selling baby food and being on hand to offer support and friendship to mothers.

Votes for Women

Barriers came down slowly and women's access to public life became more acceptable. In 1920 Henrietta Givens became Coventry's first woman magistrate, and in reporting her welcome, the *Midland Daily Telegraph* conceded that,

> For many years women have been showing their value as administrators of public affairs, and few public bodies are now composed entirely of men. The advent of Lady Astor into Parliament gave an impetus to the zeal of her sex, whose ambition to participate in local government became more pronounced.

However inspirational the election of Nancy Astor (the first woman to take her seat in the House of Commons in 1919) was, the *Midland Daily Telegraph* might also have mentioned the years of sustained campaigning by women across Britain for reforms that would bring women political, educational, social and economic equality with men. Without the passing of the Sex Disqualification (Removal) Act of 1919, women would not have entered the legal profession and Henrietta Givens would not have made it onto the bench, despite the local paper's recognition that the role was one well suited to women who could bring human sympathy, domestic knowledge and experience. And, most crucially, without the parliamentary vote, women could not take part in the democratic process by which such vital changes were made. The campaign to obtain votes for women made headline news because it included women doing things that women were not supposed to do – speaking out, refusing to be silenced, employing tactics that were disruptive, illegal and unladylike. How did it come to this?

Voices calling for women to receive the parliamentary vote grew louder and more insistent towards the end of the nineteenth century as justifications for withholding it became increasingly irrational. From 1869 single women ratepayers could vote in municipal elections and from 1894, married women also. Women could stand for election for the School Boards created by the 1870 Education Act, they could become Poor Law Guardians, but they could not vote in national elections. Increasing numbers of MPs, who relied on voteless women to fundraise and organise in their constituencies, supported the emerging suffrage groups but not in sufficient numbers to translate into legislative change, despite parliamentary efforts – bills and readings in the House – that raised, then dashed hopes. This led to increasing frustration among suffragists and determination to work for change.

In 1892 Mrs Cramp, secretary of the Coventry Women's Liberal Association asked the Coventry Liberals to support a resolution in favour of women's suffrage being discussed at the annual meeting of the National Liberal Federation. While there was some support for this, those who objected put forward arguments that were being heard up and down the country – there were more important political questions to be settled, there were 'a few ladies at the head of the movement who were undoubtedly as capable of exercising that privilege as any gentleman but [it was doubtful] whether the great majority of women were anxious that it should be conferred upon them', women were apathetic about politics and 'there were plenty of paths by which the ambitious or highly educated women of England could follow out, or work out, their destiny without going into a troublesome question like that of women's suffrage'.

A strong feeling that women should depend on their husbands to shield them from the ugly world of politics prevailed but Amy Hurlston, a member of one of Coventry's earliest suffrage groups, the Women's Emancipation Union, disagreed. At a meeting in 1895, she spoke of the exquisite irony in being told that if she got the vote she would not know what to do with it. Surely, she said, an educated woman had intelligence equal to that of the artisan and the labourer, who already had a vote. How was it that women with a municipal vote knew how to use that? The world would not be turned upside down when women got the franchise, there was no serious cause for alarm but it *was* an economic necessity, because without the vote, women workers had no power to protect themselves, they would continue to be easy prey for the sweaters of labour and this in turn would continue to drag down the wages of all workers. Women, she urged, must 'agitate, educate and cooperate'.

Deeds Not Words

In Coventry, women began to do just that. The Women's Emancipation Union of the 1890s was evidently short-lived for in 1907 the eminent scholar and historian of medieval Coventry, Mary Dormer Harris, expressed her hope that a Coventry Suffrage Society would soon form. She didn't have long to wait. Two of the most prominent suffrage organisations were represented in Coventry by 1910. The National Union of Women's Suffrage Societies (NUWSS), led nationally by Millicent Fawcett, had a Coventry branch organised by Mrs Mayer, Mrs Bright and Miss Averil Wilks. They campaigned by holding public meetings, processions and demonstrations. They were increasingly referred to in the press as the 'peaceful' part of the movement for, by 1905, the Women's Social and Political Union (WSPU – formed in Manchester in 1903 and led by Emmeline and Christabel Pankhurst) had translated frustration into direct action, with its famous motto: Deeds Not Words. Dubbed suffragettes by the press, the WSPU, like the NUWSS, organised outdoor meetings and demonstrations, but in addition, they interrupted the meetings of politicians, began a window-smashing campaign and, from 1912, militant tactics included arson, attacks on property, damage to railway stations and telegraph wires. Its members were willing to risk prison sentences and, from 1909, some convicted women undertook hunger strikes, in protest at not being categorised as political prisoners.

Much of the activism embarked on in Coventry was aimed at attracting public opinion in a time honoured political manner. During a four-day mission in the city in the spring of 1910, for example, there were lunchtime meetings outside Cash's and Rudge Whitworth, evening meetings on Pool Meadow and one morning, the main city streets were paraded by six women wearing sandwich boards advertising an event to be held that night at the Corn Exchange on Hertford Street, with Christabel Pankhurst as the principal speaker. The women included Helen Dawson, who had helped to found the Coventry branch of the WSPU in 1908 and was housekeeper (and from 1911, wife) to the Reverend Widdrington of St Peter's Church who was also a strong supporter of women's rights. It was in his Anglican parish that Coventry's first woman sidesman (usher) was elected on Easter Monday in 1912; the sidesman – Mrs Collington – was herself a committed suffrage campaigner.

One of the other sandwich-board bearers was Dorothy Evans, organiser of the Birmingham and Midlands WSPU, at whom mud was thrown as the women walked the city streets. Activists became used to much worse, both physically and verbally; in a later Coventry campaign in the spring of 1913, outdoor meetings were held on Pool Meadow, in Foleshill and Earlsdon, at which local activists were supported by organisers sent from London. The speakers endured noisy interruptions and had tufts of grass, dirt, pots, oranges and bits of wood thrown at them. The *Midland Daily Telegraph* described the crowd on Pool Meadow as 'merry' as opposed to violent but nonetheless, the women speakers had to take refuge in the Social Democratic Club in nearby White Street. Later on, two women, recognised as suffragettes while walking in Paynes Lane, were surrounded by a hostile and growing crowd of around 300 people. A man offered the women shelter in his house in Wren Street but one of his windows was broken by the mob. Police arrived to clear the area, remaining on duty until late into the night. In Earlsdon, abuse was hurled at the speakers by men and women in the crowd. Although there was some banter – 'We want blokes for women, not votes for women' – there was also rudeness – 'You don't call yourself a woman do you? You are only an apology for one' – and threats – 'Get on the platform and throw her down here'.

Some people were angered by the money spent on policing local suffrage events but in fact, as in many towns and cities, it was the loutish behaviour of crowds at both public and indoor meetings that disrupted events and made it necessary for the police to provide protection for women speakers. It was as if the militant activities of the suffragettes, as reported by the

The next three photographs show public meetings organised by the Coventry Women's Social and Political Union, probably in the spring of 1913. They were taken by John Leicester Biddle (1869-1949), a former works manager at Rudge Whitworth. *Many thanks to John Biddle and also to Damien Kimberley of Coventry History Centre for permission to use them*

The venue for this meeting is Pool Meadow. Note the Hippodrome Theatre on the left of the photograph. *Biddle, courtesy of Damien Kimberley of Coventry History Centre*

press, gave people licence to heap derision on women who, many felt, should be at home performing domestic duties rather than appearing on public platforms. In June 1908 two women wrote to the *Coventry Herald* about their experiences at a vast Hyde Park WSPU demonstration, addressed by Emmeline Pankhurst. Coventry supporters could travel by special train, leaving at 8.15 a.m. for a return fare of six and a half shillings (putting the journey out of the reach of a great many working-class women, especially those not earning much more than seven or eight shillings a week) and the two women joined an orderly procession from Kensington High Street, where the atmosphere was genial and the marchers frequently clapped by onlookers. When they reached the park, however, the atmosphere changed. At first the women thought that the jostling and pushing was due to people trying to get to the front of the crowd to hear the speakers on the platforms, but it became clear that in fact it was being done with intent to cause alarm and make mischief. At one

In this image, the woman seated in front of the wall looks anxious, quite possibly about unruly crowd behaviour, a feature of these 1913 campaign meetings. In all three photographs, the determination of the speakers to be heard by the crowd is clear. *Biddle, courtesy of Damien Kimberley of Coventry History Centre*

point the two women were pulled up onto the packed platform to offer them some protection from the crowd. It was impossible to hear the speakers as 'half the audience were quacking, some were singing and others were ringing diminutive handbells'. At the end of the meeting, a great cry of 'Votes for Women' went up and the mood of the crowd seemed to change, with hats waved and a cheer for Mrs Pankhurst.

It was reported that up to half a million people were in the park that day but similar scenes occurred at smaller Coventry gatherings. It was not only crowd ribaldry that suffrage speakers endured but political anger too. Sylvia Pankhurst and Midlands WSPU organiser Gladice Keevil faced loud opposition from a section of the audience at a meeting at Coventry's Baths Assembly Hall in the autumn of 1908. Some socialists believed that the women's suffrage organisations were mistaken in their goal of achieving suffrage for women on the same terms as it was currently for men, believing that until full adult suffrage existed in Britain, thousands of working class men and women would be excluded from the franchise because they lacked the necessary property qualifications. Political supporters and opponents clashed and speeches were interrupted by objectors as well as whirling rattles, whistles, a mouth organ, handbells, lines from popular songs and the letting off of a stink bomb. The police were called and when order was restored, Miss Pankhurst apparently looked exhausted – possibly regretting stepping in for her sister, Christabel, who was in prison – but continued with her speech, despite more interruptions. One gentleman remarked that 'we interrupted them because they do the same at "our" Ministers' meetings', a reference to the WSPU tactic of infiltrating political gatherings, unfurling Votes for Women banners and demanding to know when the government would grant women the vote. The following week, the Social Democratic Federation, which favoured adult suffrage, held a meeting at which it was made clear that despite their disagreement with the suffragettes, the disturbance at the meeting had been deplorable and the women had every right to be heard.

In order to be heard, however, and to publicly campaign, women had to display great courage. Audiences were not used to women speakers and as well as treating them as figures of fun, they used the sensational reports of militant suffragette activity as good enough reason to disrespect all women associated with the cause. When Mrs Mayer, representing the non-militant NUWSS, addressed a meeting of women and girls outside Courtaulds one lunchtime, it took her a long time to calm her excitable audience who had surged forward, laughing and shouting, nearly knocking her off her feet. When finally she managed to get them to listen, she was applauded for her statement that women's wages would rise if they got the vote, only to lose their attention again when a young man stuck his head over a hedge, yelling 'Votes for Women'. Nerves of steel and total commitment to the cause were extremely important.

The outrage expressed in the press at militancy across Britain led to some women feeling that they needed to disassociate themselves from the WSPU. At the end of her speech quoted earlier in this chapter, Selina Dix was asked if she supported the outrageous 'tricks' of the militant suffragists; the questioner wanting to clarify that, as the new NUT President, she did not sanction violent acts. Miss Dix replied that she did not. She had withdrawn her membership of the WSPU but she nevertheless reminded the audience that men had been violent when they were denied the vote and while she was not justifying what some people had done, this fact should be borne in mind when considering the acts of women who had long been thwarted in their desires. Nothing, she said, had been done for the sake of notoriety.

Away from Coventry, the city's women suffrage supporters did what they could, when they could, to try to advance the

St Peter's Fellowship, May Day 1912. Reverend PET Widdrington (second left), the Christian Socialist vicar of St Peter's Church, Hillfields, was very supportive of the suffrage cause. His wife, Helen (nee Dawson), in the light coloured coat, was a founder member of the Coventry branch of the Women's Social and Political Union and of the all -female trade union the National Federation of Women Workers. The socialist Countess of Warwick is seated. *Coventry Graphic*, 11 May 1912. *Courtesy of Coventry History Centre*

cause. In 1908 Alice Lea of 25, Queens Road, a local WSPU organiser, was arrested in London after trying to address a crowd from some railings near Westminster and was charged with obstructing the police in the execution of their duty. Refusing to pay a surety, she was sent to Holloway Prison for a month. On her release, a welcoming reception was held for her at St Peter's Vicarage, Hillfields. Reverend Widdrington said that until the vote was granted, he hoped that a 'quota of martyrs' from Coventry would go steadily to prison for 'this real living cause which means so much for the future of England'. Alice Lea said she had no regrets and went to prison because it seemed to her to be the very best way to help the movement.

Later in 1908, Miss Lettice Floyd of Berkswell, near Coventry, was arrested for riotous behaviour at Westminster. It was alleged that, as part of a delegation which had sought to present Prime Minister Asquith with a resolution, she had attempted to push her way through a cordon of police and despite being told to go back, forced her way on towards Westminster. Appearing in court with her were Emmeline Pankhurst and her daughter, Christabel, charged with failing to answer summonses for incitement, after they had been warned against distributing hand-printed bills declaring the intention to 'rush' the House of Commons. Among a large crowd, it was reported that for a short while there was a free fight in the surging mass of men, women, police and horses and there were many arrests. Whilst, on many occasions, there was police protection of women, it is fair to say that during the suffrage campaign, there were also instances of police insensitivity and even brutality towards women demonstrators. Miss Floyd, along with others, was bailed to return to court the following week, when she declined to pay a fine to be bound over and instead was taken to Holloway. There were to be further spells of imprisonment for Lettice Floyd in the following years.

Little or no violent militancy came to Coventry, although in February 1913, the *Coventry Graphic* claimed that the destructive fluid dropped into the letter box at the General Post Office, damaging letters, was the stupid, inhuman act of a

HIS MAJESTY'S MAILS.
HOW THEY WERE TREATED AT COVENTRY.

A business man's letters as they appeared after the new chemical treatment believed to have been applied by suffragettes.

The Coventry Graphic alleged that these letters were destroyed by suffragette militancy in Coventry. *Coventry Graphic*, 15 February 1913. *Courtesy of Coventry History Centre*

fanatical creature. Such acts, wrote the columnist, were 'nothing but exhibitions of advanced lunacy', and could only delay the enfranchisement of women. It was the duty of the womanhood of Coventry to subvert such behaviour. Suspicion fell on the suffragettes because, 'this knowledge of the power of chemicals has characterised [their] scientific warfare throughout the country'.

Far from being sensational, much of the activism in Coventry, as in other localities, was unglamorous and arduous. There were always requests for more women to sell newspapers and to contribute to raising campaign funds. In the winter of 1913 it was planned to open a WSPU shop to sell suffrage literature as well as homemade jams and sweets. New offices were taken at 1, Holyhead Road where tea was served every Saturday afternoon and for which the loan of a piano was gratefully received. Speakers had to be found for the weekly meeting pitch which, late in 1913, was changed from Pool Meadow to the Market Square. Sisters Harriet Collington and Dr Catherine Arnott, the WSPU's branch honorary secretary, sold their party's official newspaper every week on Broadgate.

Even this seemingly mundane task took nerve, with passers-by often making their hostility to the cause very plain. Dr Arnott, however, was made of strong stuff; on one occasion her house on Berry Street was surrounded by an angry crowd and on another, she was obliged to jump on a tram and keep travelling backwards and forwards until it was safe for her to alight. When she went down to London to take part in demonstrations, her family was never entirely sure whether they would see her that night or whether she would be spending the night in the cells.

When war was declared on 4 August 1914, Emmeline Pankhurst suspended militant campaigning and got behind the war effort, urging women to serve their country by registering for war work. Suffrage activists across the country embarked on a range of work to provide support for women affected by the war. In Coventry, members of the NUWSS were involved in the opening of a Tipperary Club in Palace Yard for the wives of soldiers and sailors. It had the use of three newly renovated rooms, comfortably furnished and supplied with newspapers, writing materials and tea and light refreshments for sale. It was open for twelve hours each day and enabled women to come and meet others, talk, relax and go on occasional outings. In May 1915 Daimler lent the Club buses so that members could go on a motor and cycling Whit Monday outing to Stratford.

In 1917 Emmeline and Christabel Pankhurst launched the strongly patriotic Women's Party, sending an organiser to Coventry in the autumn when the city's wartime production was hit by a strike over shop steward recognition, affecting up to 50,000 workers and halting production. Flora Drummond, Chief Organiser of the Women's Party, appealed to women caught up in the dispute to look at the bigger, national side of the picture, because those who had called the strike were doing nothing more than helping the enemy and were giving women's labour a bad name. The trade unions, including those representing the women workers, had agreed not to hold public meetings during the strike, but the National Federation of Women Workers objected that if the Women's Party had been given police clearance to hold talks, they would not hesitate to do so themselves and show their support for the women munition workers.

Finally, the Vote

In 1918 women over the age of 30 who met property qualifications were given the vote, amounting to about forty per cent of the total population of women. The same piece of legislation enfranchised all men over the age of 21, but it was 1928 before women from that age were also eligible to vote. There is no doubt that the suffrage campaign did an enormous amount to highlight the inequality present in the British parliamentary electorate and although there are differences of opinion about why the vote was granted in 1918 (some said it was a reward for war work – although a large number of war workers were in fact under 30; others maintained it was to prevent a return to militancy after the war, and some simply conceded that it was an inevitable step towards democracy), the sacrifices that many women made along the way were enormous, touring the country to organise and agitate, facing derision from crowds, from family and neighbours, and risking and damaging their health on repeated prison hunger strikes. The ultimate sacrifice was made by Emily Wilding Davison in 1913 when her attempt to stop the King's horse at the Epsom Derby resulted in her fatal injuries.

Women Making a Difference

Both of the Coventry women mayors in our period commented on the amount of good work that they had found going on across their city. It did not all make headline news but instead involved people endeavouring to make life better for Coventry citizens and visitors in accordance with their beliefs and in ways suited to their talents or expected of their position. This had long been the case. In May 1893, for example, the Coventry Women's Christian Temperance Association gave a tea to the 'itinerant and show people' who had come to Coventry to work at the annual fair

Raising money for Coventry hospitals on 'Alexandra Rose Day', a national fund raising day started in 1912 to mark the 50th anniversary of the arrival in Britain of Queen Alexandra, wife of King Edward Vll. *Courtesy of David Fry*

on Pool Meadow and in 1919 the Free Church Girls' Guild was trying to persuade both the Home Secretary and Coventry City Council of the importance of having a temperance booth during the peace celebrations scheduled for July. It was worried about the crowds of young people who would be thronging the streets, with all sorts of temptations, including drink, around them and so was requesting a prominent position, such as Greyfriars' Green, for the sale of cakes and non-intoxicants. To its 'grief and indignation', the request was refused but it was relieved that at least the Girls' Club would be open to members for tea.

Women gave what time they had; Mrs Rea's father was secretary of the Foleshill Philanthropic Society and as a girl, she helped out with Flag Days, collecting at some of the factories, such as the Dunlop and the Swallow (which became Jaguar) where she recalled much generosity, men often giving two or more shillings out of a weekly wage of less than £4.

Girl Guides (5th Coventry) raising money for the Red Cross. *Courtesy of David Fry*

There was continuity; the National Union of Townswomen's Guilds, formed in 1930, decided to use the colours of the suffrage organisation, the NUWSS – red for courage, white for faith and green for hope – and described itself as a modern counterpart of the women's movement, democratic, non-sectarian and non-political. The vote may have been won but the Guilds sought to offer fellowship and to develop a sense of civic consciousness among women. By 1939 there were branches in Wyken, Willenhall and Green Lane and, like the Women's Institute branches in villages such as Allesley, they raised money for the war effort, gave practical demonstrations on jam making and fruit bottling, on making the most of available foods and on learning not just how to Dig For Victory but to grow vegetables successfully.

Women's work was not always aimed at making a political, social or even practical difference. Two prominent local women – author Angela Brazil and historian Mary Dormer Harris – were

The official opening of the Coventry Guild Museum, in the Old Bablake School, Hill Street, 1920. *Courtesy of Coventry History Centre*

centrally involved in the creation of the Coventry City Guild in 1914, aimed at preserving Coventry's 'ancient and modern beauties' and drawing up a schedule of buildings worthy of preservation. In 1920 they were part of the committee that realised an ambition to open a museum, displaying articles of local historic interest which had been donated by members of the public. By the early 1920s the museum was housed in the Old Bablake School and opened its doors every day.

Postscript: Life in 1950 and Beyond

There is nearly another seventy years of the history of women's lives in Coventry still to write. For now we leave the story with the election of Coventry's first woman Member of Parliament, Elaine Burton, in 1950, with peace restored in Britain and with Coventry known worldwide for its spirited determination to overcome adversity after the devastating air raids of 1940 and 1941. In 1943, Coventry's mayor, Emily Smith, was presented with an address from the Women of Stalingrad to the Women of Coventry, declaring solidarity with 'our valiant sisters, daughters of the great English people', who had worked without

Some of Coventry's first post war new housing on the Monks Park estate, Holbrooks, built in 1947. *Municipal Tenants' Handbooks. Courtesy of Coventry History Centre*

The dining room of a new Council house on the Barnfield Estate, Allesley, built in 1949. *Municipal Tenants' Handbooks. Courtesy of Coventry History Centre*

rest, 'producing armaments to bring nearer the hour of victory over our common foe, the foe of humanity'. Many of those valiant sisters would have looked on with interest in 1946 at the Levelling Stone placed by the City Council at the top of what later became the Upper Precinct. Made of slate with a central bronze Phoenix rising from the ashes, it commemorates the official inauguration of the rebuilding of Coventry and remains today at the top of the Upper Precinct. For a while longer, the prefabs, the rationing and the drabness of post-war life would continue but change was afoot and women and men would go forward to make the best of the new opportunities presented and be joined by thousands of newcomers, eager to live and work in this city with its vision of hope and inclusiveness. As in the hundred years of this book, there would be good times and bad, industrial collapse and economic reinvention, social change and political challenges. Throughout, women have – and will – continue to be involved in all aspects of the city's life and I am proud to be among them.

Bibliography

Coventry History Centre

Atkins, Rosa E., 1871 School Exercise book PA/1087/16/2

Board of Trade: Cost of Living of the Working Classes (Coventry) 1912 AB331.831

Board of Trade Report on Increased Employment of Women during the War PA2567/13/1

Bray, Charles, *The Industrial Employment of Women*, Longman, 1857

The Builder 1862 JN614.8

Census materials, England and Wales 1851-1931

Chauntry Clearance Area, Ministry of Health Inquiry 1934

Chief Constable Reports 1919-68 JN352.2

City of Coventry Annual Reports on the Health of the City, 1889-1950

City of Coventry: First Annual Report of the Distress Committee established under the Unemployed Workman Act 1905 JN331.137

City of Coventry Public Health Department (Local Notes from Better Health 1929-40) JN614

Coventry Certified Industrial School, CCF/6/6/1

Coventry City Council Sanitary Committee Minutes 1919-31 CCA/1/4/18/1/10

Coventry Co-operative Society Jubilee History 1867-1917, JN 334.06

Coventry Directories

Coventry Industrial School and Home for Girls PA606

Coventry *Local History Bulletin* 1983-6 JN905

Coventry Municipal Yearbooks

Coventry Provident Society Annual Reports JN362.12

Coventry Sentinel Cuttings 1908-10 JN335 (Votes for Women Mission)

Coventry Union Board of Guardian Minutes 1896-1898 SLA/6/1/17-19

Coventry Union Parishes Board of Directors 1869-1873 SLA/6/1/7 & SLA/6/1/14 from 1888

Coventry Union Poor Law Guardian Admissions and Discharge Books SLA/6/13

Coventry & Warwickshire Hospital Reports 1865-1944 JN362

Dix, Selina anonymous, undated, unpublished biography, 1859-1942 PA1344/20

Domestic Economy Exercise Book, 1942, PA1906/7

Free Church Girls Guild PA2679/1/8

Girls' Friendly Society 1913-28 PA888

Heaviside's Books of Newspaper Cuttings JN080

Higher Education Special Committee Minute Book CCA/1/4/27/8/1

Hospital Saturday Fund Minute Book ACC NO

James, Ann 'Children At School: A Collection of Documents to Illustrate Education in Coventry in the 18th and 19th Centuries'

The Jubilee Year of the Coventry Ragged Schools 1897

Lowe's Cuttings

The Microcosm (Stoke Park School Magazine)

Midland History Journal 1971-2014

Midwives Registers PA63/1 1847-1872; 1858-1866; 1866-1875

National Council of Women: 40 Years of Women's Work in Coventry 1917-1957, PA1269/7/1

Record of Blue Coat by Mrs E Masterman PA1037/112/2-3

Red Lane Social History Project PA1235

Report of Inspection of the Girls' Pupil Teacher Centre, February 1908, CCE/SCH/15/3/5

St Faiths' Annual Reports and Committee Meetings CCF/2

St Faith's Shelter Reports 1922-68 362.72

St John's Girls and Infant School 1900-24 Log Book CCE/LOG/4/6-7

South Street School Log Book CCE/LOG/8/4

Spon Street Girls School Log Book 1873-1900 CCE/LOG/6/3-4

Stevenson, Lily, Admission as a Freeman of Coventry PA660

Vita Nuova (Barr's Hill School Magazine)

Wheatley Street Girls School Log Book CCE/LOG/20/3-4

Women's Land Army general correspondence and papers CCB/3/1/54

Women's Voluntary Service PA1753/2/1-140

Oral Histories at Coventry Archives

Oral History Project

PA1662/2/9 W. Wilson

PA/1662/2/17 Mrs N. Dingley

PA/1662/2/46 Mrs E. Simmons

PA/1662/2/48 Mrs Lee

PA/1662/2/54 Mrs Brown

PA/1662/2/60 Mrs Bucknell

PA/1662/2/62 Mrs Rea

PA/1662/2/74 Mrs F. Emes

PA/1662/2/117

PA/1662/2/131

PA/1662/2/149 Mrs Rollaston

PA/1662/2/155 Mrs Purnell

PA/1662/2/161

PA/1662/3/24 Mrs Delia Fell

PA/1662/3/29 Miss F. Barton

PA/1662/3/48 M. W. M. Barnes

From the Car Workers' Project:

PA1647/1/5

PA1647/1/6

PA/1647/1/21

PA/1647/1/33

PA/1647/1/35

PA/1647/1/36

PA/1647/1/39

Other archives and collections:

BBC Listener Reports https://microform.digital/boa/collections/16/bbc-listener-research-department-reports-1937-c1950

Coventry Trade Council Annual Reports 1895-7, 1914 Modern Record Centre, University of Warwick MSS.5/4/AN

Gertrude Tuckwell 'Reminiscences', Gertrude Tuckwell Papers, TUC Library Collections, London Metropolitan University

Herbert Art Gallery & Museum, Coventry; photograph collection

Imperial War Museum, London: Women, War and Society 1914–18; Sound Archive (Elsie Farlow) Sound Archive

Interviews Bill Wilson and Cathy Hunt 1999 & 2001. *Author's own*

Report on Industrial Welfare Conditions in Coventry, Advisory Committee on Women's War Employment, 1916, Imperial War Museum, EMP.45.7 IWM

Report of the Royal Commission on the Aged Poor, Volume 2, 1895, British Library

Kenneth Richardson tapes (W Wilson), Coventry University Lanchester Library

Newspapers and Journals

Alfred Herbert News

The Builder

Coventry Graphic (CG)

Coventry Herald (CH)

Coventry Sentinel

Coventry Standard (CS)

Coventry Times (CT)

Illustrated

Leamington Spa Courier

The Loudspeaker

Midland Daily Telegraph (MDT) (became *Coventry Evening Telegraph*)

The Rayoneer

The Suffragette

Votes for Women

Warwick & Warwickshire and Leamington Gazette

The Wheatsheaf

Woman Worker

Women's Trade Union Review

Worcester Journal

Workers' Union Record

Coventry Women's Research Group publications, for research on:

Barbara Davies, Evelyn Evans, Selina Dix, Beatrice Callow, Dorothy Parker, Megan Saxelby, Janet Done, Lily Stevenson, Gwendoline Smith, Edith Atkins, Margery Evans

From *Redressing the Balance*, 1999

Hurdy Gurdy Days, 2001

Keeping the Balance, 2001

Telling Tales, 2003

Making the Best of Things, 2007

Against All Odds, 2011

Some additional references relating to individual women and stories mentioned in the text

Alice Arnold, 20 January 1945 *MDT;* Cathy Hunt, *A Woman of the People*

Gertrude Beamish, VAD, http://www.redcross.org.uk/en/About-us/Who-we-are/History-and-origin/First-World-War

Mary Beardsall, 16 August 1941 *CS*

Mrs Bonham and Mrs Carter, tram strike 8 February 1918, *MDT*

Margaret Brown, George Medal 5 July 1941 *MDT*

Joyce Burton, 5 July 1941 *MDT*

Frances Power Cobbe in Barbara Caine, *Victorian Feminists*, Oxford University Press, 1992

Coventry Domestic Service after the First World War, *Woman Worker,* February 1919

Coventry suffrage: Lettice Floyd, 23 October 1908, *Morning Post*; Alice Lea 8 July 1908 MDT and *Votes for Women*; memories of Mrs Collington and Dr Arnott 13 February

1939, *MDT;* Selina Dix speech, *CS* 6/7 March 1914; Liberals on suffrage, *MDT* 21 Oct 1892; Amy Hurlston, 2 March 1895, *Worcester Journal*; Hyde Park, *Coventry Herald*, 27 June 1908; Spring campaign, 30/1 May 1913; *MDT*, 18 November 1908, 25 November 1908; *Coventry Sentinel; The Suffragette*; Courtaulds meeting 2 May 1910 MDT, Women's Party, *MDT*, 1 December 1917

Coventry VAD nurses Annie Elizabeth Cramp, Olive Mary Reynolds, http://www.redcross.org.uk/en/About-us/Who-we-are/History-and-origin/First-World-War

Ada Curtis, 6 July 1917 *MDT*

Education in the 1850s, 25 April 1851, 19 March 1852, *CH*

Henrietta Givens, Coventry's First Woman Magistrate, 23 Sept 1920, *MDT*; Cathy Hunt, *The National Federation of Women Workers, 1906–21*

Sarah Griffiths, 30 May 1952, *Coventry Evening Telegraph; The Woman Worker, 1908*

Grace Howell, 14 November 1940, *MDT* obituary

Dr Elsie Humpherson speech at Warwick High School, *Warwick Advertiser & Leamington Gazette*, 29 June 1929

Amy Hurlston, 'The Factory Work of Women in the Midlands', *Women's Emancipation Union Publications*, 1893; Royal Commission on the Aged Poor, 1895, HMSO, *Coventry Poor Law Union Guardian Minute Books* CT, *Birmingham Daily Post, Worcester Journal, Sheffield Daily Telegraph,* Lowe's Cuttings (Coventry Archives)

Nurse Harriet Ives, 21 May 1952, *MDT*

Florence Jackson, *Red Lane Reminiscences*, 1983

Florence Johnson, 15 February 1918, *CS*

Evelyn Jones, in Mavis Nicholson, *What Did You Do In The War, Mummy?*

Mona Jones, Wartime Memories, from Tim Lewis, *Moonlight Sonata*

Elizabeth Moorcroft, Coventry Union Parishes Board of Directors SLA/6/1/7

Nurses commended to Secretary of State, 5 March 1917, *MDT*

OBEs for Women factory workers in the First World War, 18 November 1918, *Birmingham Daily Post*

Emily Penrose speech (1908 opening of Barr's Hill), *Vita Nuova*

Mrs Dr Potts 8 June 1894 *CH*

Althea Seymour, VAD http://www.redcross.org.uk/en/About-us/Who-we-are/History-and-origin/First-World-War

Lucy Sly, 30 Jan 1889 *CT*

Emily Smith, 7 November 1942; 8 February 1943; 4 November 1943, *MDT*

Stoke Park Victory in Europe quote, *Microcosm*

Wedding of Gertrude Langley and Walter Beamish 9 September 1914, *MDT*

Women Police in the First World War 13 July 1917, *MDT*, 2 March 1917, *CS*

Workers' Birth Control Group, Angela Holdsworth, *Out of the Doll's House; the Story of Women in the Twentieth Century*

Websites

Ancestry https://www.ancestry.co.uk/

British Newspaper Archive http://www.britishnewspaperarchive

British Red Cross http://www.redcross.org.uk/About-us/Who-we-are/History-and-origin/First-World-War/Volunteers-during-WW1

Coventry Now and Then (for information about Coventry theatres and cinemas) *https://www.historiccoventry.co.uk*

Coventry Transport Museum, Muriel Hind http://wiki.transport-museum.com/Default.aspx?Page=Muriel%20Hind&AspxAutoDetectCookieSupport=1

Education in England, text of the Taunton Commissionhttp://www.educationengland.org.uk/documents/sicr/sicr1-06.html

Girls' Industrial Home, Coventry, Warwickshire, http://www.childrenshomes.org.uk/CoventryIS/

Heritage Lottery Funded Project, 'No Game for Girls' https://www.youtube.com/watch?v=V-ETBTtnlX4

Workhouse http://www.workhouses.org.uk/Coventry/

Selected Secondary sources

Adams, Kathleen, *The Chronicles of Barr's Hill House 1850-1982*, 1983, 942.48, Nuneaton Borough Council, 1970

Alexander, Sally, *Becoming a Woman and Other Essays in 19th and 20th Century Feminist* History, New York University Press, 1995

Andrews, William, unpublished Diary and Joseph Gutteridge, Autobiography*; Master and Artisan in Victorian England,* Evelyn, Adams and Mackay, 1969

Badger, Frances J., 'Illuminating Nineteenth Century English Urban Midwifery: the Register of a Coventry Midwife' in *Women's History Review*, volume 23, number 5, 2014

Braybon, Gail & Summerfield Penny, *Out of the Cage: Women's Experiences in Two World Wars*, Pandora, 1987

Caine, Barbara, *Victorian Feminists*, Oxford University Press, 1992

Calder, Angus, *The People's War: Britain, 1939–45*, Pimlico, 1969

Castle, Eileen, *Coventry At School*, Coventry Archives 1997

Cowman, Krista, *Women of the Right Spirit: Paid Organisers of the Women's Social and Political Union (WSPU) 1904–18*, Manchester University Press, 2007

Crawford, Elizabeth, *The Women's Suffrage Movement, A Reference Guide 1866–1928,* Routledge, 1999

Demidowicz, George, *A History of the Blue Coat School and the Lych Gate Cottages, Coventry*, Coventry City Council 2000

Dodge, Jenny, *Silken Weave; Ribbon Making in Coventry*, Herbert Art Gallery & Museum, 1986

Dyhouse, Carol, *Girls Growing Up in Late Victorian and Edwardian England*, Routledge & Kegan Paul, 1981

Eliot, George, *Middlemarch*, Penguin, 1873

Field, Rachel, *Ipswich in the Great War*, Pen and Sword Ltd, 2016

Firth, Geoffrey C., *75 Years of Service to Education*, Coventry Education Committee 1977, Coventry Archives

Forster, Margaret, *Significant Sisters: The Grassroots of Active Feminism 1839–1939*, Penguin, 1984

Freeman-Cuerden, Caroline, *Veterans' Voices: Coventry's Unsung Heroes of the Second World War*, The History Press, 2005

Gaffin, Jean & David Thoms, *Caring and Sharing: the Centenary History of the Co-operative Women's Guild,* Co-Ooperative Union, 1983

Gardiner, Juliet, *The Thirties: An Intimate History*, Harper Press, 2010

Hall, Rosemary, 'Distressed Weavers, Deserted Wives and Fever Cases; an Analysis of Admissions to Coventry Workhouse, 1859–81', *Warwickshire History*, Winter 2007/8

Hillfields History Group, *Hillfields in their Own Words; Life and Work in the Home*,

Hockton, Lynn, *Skid; A Coventry Childhood*, 2003

Holdsworth, Angela, *Out of the Doll's House; the Story of Women in the Twentieth Century*, BBC Books, 1988 – source for quote about dangers of childbirth compared with mining

Hollis, Patricia, *Ladies Elect: Women in English Local Government 1865–1914,* Clarendon Press 1987

Holloway, Gerry, *Women and Work in Britain since 1840*, Routledge, 2005

Hughes, Kathryn, *George Eliot, The Last Victorian*, Fourth Estate, 1999

Hunt, Cathy, *A Woman of the People: Alice Arnold of Coventry 1881–1955*, Coventry Historical Association, 2007

Hunt, Cathy, *The National Federation of Women Workers, 1906–1921*, Palgrave Macmillan, 2014

Hylands, Ivy, *My Life as a Blue Coat Girl* Athena Press, 2007

Lancaster, Bill & Mason, Tony (eds), *Life and Labour in a Twentieth Century City: The Experience of Coventry,* Cryfield Press, 1986

Lethbridge, Lucy, *Servants: A Downstairs View of 20th century Britain*, Bloomsbury, 2013

Lewis, Jane, *Women in England, 1870–1950*, Harvester Wheatsheaf, 1984

Lewis, Tim, *Moonlight Sonata*, Lewis & Coventry City Council, 1990

Llewelyn Davies, Margaret, (ed) *Maternity: Letters from Working Women*, (first published 1915), Virago, 1978

Marks, Lara, *Metropolitan Maternity; Maternal and Infant Welfare Services in Early Twentieth Century London,* Rodopi, 1996

McIntosh, Tania, *Social History of Maternity and Childbirth: Key Themes in Maternity Care*, Routledge, 2012 (source of information about Florence Nightingale's model lying in hospital p.28)

Nakamura, Nobuko, 'Women, Work and War: Industrial Mobilisation and Demobilisation, Coventry and Bolton 1940-46', unpublished PhD thesis, University of Warwick, 1984

Nicholson, Mavis, *What Did You Do In The War, Mummy?* Seren Books, 1995

Nightingale, Florence, 'Cassandra' in Ray Strachey, *The Cause; A Short History of the Women's Movement in Great Britain,* Virago, 1978 (first published 1928)

Pember Reeves, Maud, *Round About A Pound A Week*, Virago, 1999 (first published 1913)

Prest, John, *The Industrial Revolution in Coventry*, Oxford University Press, 1960

Priestley, J.P., *An English Journey*, Victor Gollancz, 1934

Purvis, June (ed), *Women's History: Britain 1850–1945,* UCL, 1995

Red Lane Reminiscences, printed by Coventry Resource and Information Service, 1983

Richardson, Kenneth, *Twentieth Century Coventry*, City of Coventry 1972

Roberts Elizabeth, *Women's Work, 1840–1940*, Cambridge University Press, 1988

Ross, Ellen, *Love and Toil: Motherhood in Outcast London, 1870–1918,* Oxford University Press, 1993

Rubenstein, David, 'Cycling in the 1890s', in *Victorian Studies*, Volume 21, number 1 1977

Searby, Peter, 'The Relief of the Poor in Coventry, 1830–1863' in *The Historical Journal*, 20,2 1977

Smith, Albert & David Fry, *Godiva's Heritage: Coventry's Industry*, Simanda Press, 1997

Smith, Frederick, *Coventry: 600 Years of Municipal Life*, City of Coventry 1945

Smith, Janet Frances, *Labour: Having a Baby Before the Birth of the NHS*, JAY Publishing, 1997 Smith, D.J.H., (Compiled) *Coventry Through the Ages, 1540-1934,* Coventry and County Heritage (HA), 1993

Stevenson, John, *British Society 1914-45*, Penguin, 1984

Stoke Park History Group, 'The House in the Park: the Story of Stoke Park School'

Strack, Birgit, 'Labour Politics in Coventry 1890–1914', unpublished MA thesis, University of Warwick, 1990

Thane, Pat, 'Women and the Poor Law in Victorian and Edwardian England' in *History Workshop Journal,* Volume 6, issue 1, 1978

Tiratsoo, Nicholas, 'Coventry's Ribbon Trade in the Mid-Victorian period', unpublished PhD thesis, University of London, 1980

Turner, Mary, *The Women's Century: A Celebration of Changing Roles, 1900–2000*, National Archives, 2003

Victoria History of the Counties of England; *A History of Warwickshire*, Volume 8, University of London, Institute of Historical Research, 1969

Walters, Peter (in association with Culture Coventry), *Coventry: Remembering 1914–18*, The History Press, 2016

Woolacott, Angela, *On Her Their Lives Depend: Munitions Workers in the Great War*, University of California Press, 1994

Wright, Maureen, 'The Women's Emancipation Union and Radical Feminist Politics in Britain, 1891–99', in *Gender and History*, volume 22, no 2 2010

Yates, John, *Pioneers to Power*, Coventry Labour Party, 1950

Index